**Praise for Pi**

"Hendrickson does a yeoman's job demonstrating that Piketty's book is not about capital, as its name would suggest. Instead, it is an attack on free markets and personal liberty and a prescription for more government."

*-Walter E. Williams*
John M. Olin Distinguished Professor of Economics
George Mason University

"Hendrickson has written a terrific book—insightful, timely, and well written. As the new Congress considers tax reform, I hope every Member will read it."

*-Diana Furchtgott-Roth*
Senior Fellow and Director, Economics21
Manhattan Institute for Policy Research

"Hendrickson has spared us from having to read Piketty's old, tired redistributionist arguments and from having to plod through all of its bungled statistics, refuted data, and confusion of cause and effect."

*-Charles Goyette*
Author of *The Dollar Meltdown*

"Mark Hendrickson's analysis is essential reading for anyone who wants to understand not just why Piketty has misfired in his critique of capitalism, but also why the inequality he decries is an intensively positive sign that the individual liberty driving all human advancement has not yet been suffocated by the political class."

*-John Tamny*
RealClearMarkets Editor; Author of *Dollars and Sense*

1

"Mark Hendrickson is a brilliant economist. His review of Piketty's influential tome is superb and badly needed. This is an impressive and important work, packing a lot of wallop into a small space."

*-Paul Kengor*
Author of *11 Principles of a Reagan Conservative*

"In his extended review of Thomas Piketty's *Capital*, Mark Hendrickson provides us with a serious and thorough analysis and refutation of the lacunae, pitfalls, and arguments of the most exhaustive attempt to bolster a failing egalitarianism in modern times."

*-Fr. Robert Sirico*
President and Co-founder of The Acton Institute

"A valuable contribution to a valuable debate that must take place for the sake of our political future."

*-Amity Shlaes*
Calvin Coolidge Presidential Foundation

"Hendrickson demolishes the myth that Piketty has penned some sort of powerful manifesto. It turns out to be little more than gobbledygook wrapped in balderdash and surrounded with nonsense."

*-Lawrence W. Reed*
President, Foundation for Economic Education

"Hendrickson has written a classic for our time—a devastating critique of a modern reincarnation of Marxist political economy. This book can be compared to the demolition of Marxist theory by Eugen Böhm-Bawerk."

*-Yuri N. Maltsev*
Author of *Requiem for Marx*

# Problems with Piketty: The Flaws and Fallacies in *Capital in the Twenty-First Century*

By Mark Hendrickson

# The Center for Vision & Values

*America is exceptional because its foundation rests on truth. The passionate pursuit and defense of that truth is the quest of The Center for Vision & Values at Grove City College as we seek to create a dynamic learning community to connect, educate and empower people to strengthen the faith and freedom foundation of American citizenship and advance liberty around the world.*

*At The Center for Vision & Values, we view a love for truth and a love for liberty as inseparable allies. Liberty cannot long flourish in the absence of truth, and truth is not affirmed where liberty is denied. In fact, America's extraordinary achievement lies in the essential combination of both truth and liberty. Our love for liberty reflects an historic affirmation of truth in our founding documents and in our laws. Consequently, understanding the relationship between God's truth and our liberty is not merely an academic exercise, but a vital privilege of Christian stewardship.*

The Center for Vision & Values @ Grove City College

ISBN-13: 978-1503145214
ISBN-10: 1503145212

Copyright © 2014 The Center for Vision & Values

Requests for information should be mailed to:
The Center for Vision & Values, 100 Campus Drive, Grove City, PA 16127

Cover design: Churchill Strategies.

# Acknowledgements

"No man is an island," wrote the English metaphysical poet, John Donne. I'm especially mindful of that profound truth as this book goes to print. While writing is a solitary activity, the fact is that many people other than myself have made this book possible.

I'd like to thank all my teachers, but particularly Ted Walters, who taught me how to write, and the late economist, Hans F. Sennholz, who taught me how to reason economically, just as his mentor, Ludwig von Mises, had taught him.

I salute three colleagues at the Center for Vision & Values: Paul Kengor, executive director and one of the pre-eminent Cold War and Reagan scholars in the world, who somehow finds time to encourage me in spite of a prodigious workload—teaching college, publishing books and articles at a dizzying pace, while helping his wife raise seven children; Lee Wishing, administrative director, who first asked me to write a review of Piketty's book, then agreed to let me write this more thorough critique and then provided expert editorial guidance in arranging the chapters; and Robert Rider, media relations director, who expressed great patience and professionalism in support of this book project, even taking it upon himself to take a crash course in book production. All three of these men are not just helpful colleagues, but true friends.

Much gratitude goes go to the Board of Trustees of Grove City College and numerous donors who so generously support the Center for Vision & Values.

Their contributions are indispensable as the Center strives to uphold the traditional values of faith and freedom that have so greatly blessed and will continue to bless our country.

My humble and heartfelt thanks go to the esteemed and highly accomplished scholars who were more than kind and generous in offering endorsements of this book: Diana Furchtgott-Roth, Charles Goyette, Paul Kengor, Arthur Laffer, Yuri Maltsev, Ron Paul, Larry Reed, Amity Shlaes, Fr. Robert Sirico, John Tamny, and Walter Williams.

Most importantly, let me acknowledge the two loves of my life, Eileen and Karin, who make all the work worthwhile.

And finally, thank you, dear reader, for caring enough about the well-being of humanity and the future of our country and world to take the time to consider the lessons in this book. If you find any shortcomings herein, the responsibility is entirely mine.

Mark Hendrickson
November 2014

# Table of Contents

7

## *Foreword*

Like his mentor, the great Austrian economist Dr. Hans Sennholz, Dr. Mark Hendrickson has a special talent for being able to explain complex economic matters in simple and engaging prose. So, when Thomas Piketty's "Capital in the Twenty-First Century" took the world by storm, we asked him to write an opinion editorial explaining Piketty's thinking. Mark responded that he would need to write a book review to treat Piketty fairly and to do an adequate job for his readers. A few weeks later, he turned in a comprehensive review. We believe Hendrickson's work is far more than a book review, it's a compact educational resource tool for professors, journalists, economists, politicians, think tank operatives and anyone who wants to understand the tension between free market capitalism and progressive, statist economic views. We believe you'll enjoy Hendrickson's refreshing, understandable writing style. And, please note that the table of contents will serve as a quick reference guide to Hendrickson's concise analyses of Piketty's multi-faceted thought. We think it's likely you'll be quoting Mark Hendrickson for years to come.

*Lee Wishing III,* administrative director, The Center for Vision & Values at Grove City College

**A note to the reader**: This extended review may contain more than you ever wanted to know about "Capital in the Twenty-First Century." Because this book has become a bestseller and has important political implications, I have included a fairly lengthy discussion of what the consequences would be of acting on Piketty's theories and recommendations. Everything from the author's style to his biases to the subtle and not-so-subtle economic fallacies embedded in the text have been critiqued, analyzed, and unmasked so that the reader may be better equipped to understand the thrust of this blockbuster. I have written it both for laymen who are interested in politics, economics, and public policy, as well as for college students and fellow college professors who may not have time to read in their entirety the nearly 700 pages of this much-talked-about book.--M.H.

# Part One:
# The political context
# of the book

## Introduction

Since the publication of its English translation in March 2014, "Capital in the Twenty-First Century" by French economist Thomas Piketty has become a political blockbuster, an "unlikely bestseller,"[1] in the words of "The Economist." Interestingly, "Cap21" (if you don't mind my abbreviation) has made a much bigger splash in the USA than it did in France last year when its French-language original was published. Why?

A blogger at "The Economist" conjectures that Mr. Piketty's book, in which he argues for a global wealth tax to lessen income inequality and reduce the concentration of capital within and between countries, was too moderate in tone and too tame in policy recommendations to enthuse Europe's zealous leftist intellectuals.[2] The latter would have preferred a more strident, bombastic all-out assault against capitalism.[3] Indeed, the far left must have been disappointed by the modest concessions Piketty made to private property and free markets, such as: "there is no obvious reason to think that nearly all needs should by [sic; "be"] paid for through taxes" (page 482) and that the "optimal tax rate in the developed countries is probably above 80 percent" (page 512) rather than 100 percent. Piketty's

---

[1] Thomas Piketty's "Capital", summarized in four paragraphs, May 4, 2014; www.economist.com/blogs/economist-explains/2014/05/economist-explains.
[2] "Le French Touch," by S.P., April 28, 2014; www.economist.com/blogs/charlemagne/2014/04/thomas-piketty?fsrc=explainsdig.
[3] David Harvey, "Afterthoughts on Piketty's Capital," May 18, 2014; www.socialistworker.org/blog/critical-reading/2014/05/18/david-harvey-reviews-thomas-pi.

overall thesis that government should exercise a lot more control over a country's wealth is very much mainstream and uncontroversial in France.[4] Here in the States, by contrast, Piketty's policy recommendations are controversial, and controversy generates publicity.

Given our current political tensions, it is easy to see why "Cap21" has made such a big splash here. From the president of the United States, outgoing Senate Majority Leader Harry Reid, House Minority Leader Nancy Pelosi and their partisans in Congress to their intellectual allies, such as influential New York Times columnist Paul Krugman[5] and his fellow Nobel economist Robert Solow,[6] American progressives have found a kindred spirit in Thomas Piketty. By advocating higher tax rates on the rich, a global tax on wealth made possible by international cooperation that strips away all financial privacy (the NSA on steroids?), and increased redistribution designed to reduce economic inequality, Piketty is an ideological soul mate of American progressives, the economist from central casting who is perfect for the role of "economic superstar." Progressive campaign teams can cite him in upcoming election years and beyond.

---

[4] Pascal-Emmanuel Gobry, ""A Not-So-Radical French Thinker," The Wall Street Journal, May 24-25, 2014, p. C3.
[5] Paul Krugman, "The Piketty Panic," The New York Times, April 24, 2014; www.nytimes.com/2014/04/25/opinion/krugman-the-piketty-panic.html?_r=0.
[6] Robert M. Solow, "Thomas Piketty Is Right," The New Republic, April 22, 2014; www.newrepublic.com/article/117429/capital-twenty-first-century-thomas-piketty-reviewed.

Think about it: For a respected European economist to come out with a lengthy treatise containing mounds of data that, it is claimed, prove that government must play a greater role in the distribution of wealth is, if not manna from heaven, at the very least fortuitous timing for American progressives. The parallels between the American release of "Cap21" this year to the publication of John Maynard Keynes' "The General Theory of Employment, Interest, and Money" in the winter of 1935-36 are striking.

Both books came out after five or six years of economic sluggishness. In each case, the incumbent president desired an expansion of government involvement in the economy as his proposed solution for improving economic conditions. Now, as then, a Big Government president was having a hard time convincing a divided public, weary of years of economic sluggishness, that his policies would revitalize the economy. In both cases, a European economist seemingly came out of nowhere with a weighty book essentially endorsing the incumbent's policy agenda and purporting to prove that the administration's desired policies are correct, necessary, and just. Keynes became the toast of the town to Big Government progressives in the mid-30s and Piketty has achieved similar popularity and status among progressives today.

Demonstrating Mark Twain's adage that history doesn't repeat itself, but sometimes rhymes, one significant difference between the 1930s and today is that when Keynes's book came out in favor of government running large budget deficits to combat economic stagnation, the administrations of Presidents Hoover and Roosevelt already had been running deficits for over five years. Today, by contrast, the global wealth tax advocated by Piketty has been on President Obama's wish list from Day One, but has not been enacted or implemented. In both cases, though, the European rock star economist has recommended policies ill-suited to economic recovery. Keynes's policy of prescription for government deficit spending hadn't brought about recovery in the five-plus years that the policy had been in effect when his book was published, and the deficit spending that continued, both in peacetime and war, in the ten years following the "General Theory's" publication, likewise failed to produce an economic recovery. Similarly today, Piketty's recommended policies of higher taxes would, if implemented, retard economic recovery today. (Even Keynes, an advocate of government intervention to "fix" the economy, believed that higher taxes would hinder recovery.)

If the same dynamic plays out today that played out in the 1930s, actual economic results will be irrelevant to Piketty's popularity. American progressives will embrace, promote, praise, and attempt to canonize him for providing them with an urgently needed political fig leaf—an intellectual justification for the progressives' economically counterproductive policy preferences. The timing of Piketty's "Cap21" is as opportune as the timing of Keynes' "General Theory." It will be interesting to see, over the coming years, if Piketty can match the longevity of Keynes' popularity.[7]

_____

[7] The enduring popularity of Keynes may be the eighth wonder of the world. Government deficit spending during the Great Depression was ineffectual (as it has been under

## Piketty's magic trick – focusing the debate on income inequality

The central theme of Thomas Piketty's "Cap21" is that incomes and accumulated wealth are distributed very unequally, both within countries and between countries. He laments the historical fact that "no society has ever existed in which ownership of capital can reasonably be described as 'mildly' inegalitarian" (page 258). Further, "The distribution of capital ownership ... is always more concentrated than the distribution of income from labor" (page 244). Foremost among his stated goals is his desire to change "the distribution of capital ownership which is extremely inegalitarian everywhere" (page 257, accompanying table page 248).

Piketty devotes much of "Cap21" to measuring trends in the capital-to-income ratio, citing voluminous data in support of his contention that current trends are unsustainable and worrisome. American progressives have enthusiastically embraced the book's premise and

George W. Bush and Barack Obama) yet Keynes was lionized. When economic journalist Henry Hazlitt analyzed Keynes's "General Theory" chapter by chapter in his 1959 book "The Failure of the 'New Economics,'" he found that "What is original in the book is not true; and what is true is not original" (page 6). Keynesian doctrines lost prestige in the 1970s when "stagflation" (simultaneous high unemployment and high inflation) occurred despite the Keynesian doctrine that such a combination was impossible. However, in the 2000s, in a desperate attempt to rationalize larger government deficits, Keynes was dusted off and rehabilitated. See Mark W. Hendrickson, "The Ghost of John Maynard Keynes, March 13, 2009; The Center for Vision & Values; www.visionandvalues.org/2009/03/the-ghost-of-john-maynard-keynes/

policy prescriptions. Not surprisingly, there has been considerable pushback from those opposed to the Piketty/progressive higher-taxes, more-redistribution agenda.

The bulk of the pushback has consisted of challenges to the validity of the data cited in "Cap21." Indeed, throughout the book, Piketty repeatedly invited and encouraged such a debate. Here is a small sample of the disagreements with Piketty's data:

• Harvard's Martin Feldstein, a former chairman of the president's Council of Economic Advisors, wrote persuasively that "Piketty's Numbers Don't Add Up"[8] because they ignore changes in tax laws and omit income received from government transfer payments, including Social Security.

• American Enterprise Institute's Kevin A. Hassett and Aparna Mathur maintain that inequality is more accurately measured by looking at consumption rather than stated incomes.[9]

• The blogosphere is full of challenges and rebuttals to Piketty, a worthy example being Scott Winship's blog

---

[8] Martin Feldstein, "Piketty's Numbers Don't Add Up," The Wall Street Journal, May 15, 2014, page A15; www.online.wsj.com/news/articles/SB10001424052702304 081804579557664176917086.
[9] Cf. Kevin A. Hassett & Aparna Mathur, "Consumption and the Myths of Inequality; Mathur, "The Inequality Illusion"; Mathur, "Income Inequality in the United States, all in "Opportunity for All: How to Think about Income Inequality," American Enterprise Institute (no copyright date).

on Forbes.com. Winship cites multiple measuring errors, such as the omission of employer-provided benefits (e.g., healthcare insurance) and non-taxable capital gains (e.g., appreciation in house prices in the decades before 2008), the inclusion of distorting factors like "teenagers with summer jobs and undergraduates with work-study positions," and a failure to adjust data to account for reductions in the number of people per household.[10]

● Perhaps best known, "The Financial Times" ripped Piketty, asserting, "in his spreadsheets, however, there are transcription errors from original sources and incorrect formulas. It also appears that some of the data are cherry-picked or constructed without an original source… Once the FT cleaned up and simplified the data, the European numbers do not show any tendency towards rising wealth inequality after 1970."[11] Winship, by the way, despite having his own disagreements with Piketty, does not completely agree with the FT's number-crunching either.

● Responding to the FT criticisms, Piketty made a startling concession: He retracted the data in "Cap21" that he used to quantify wealth inequality in the US. In its place, Piketty claims that data gathered by economists Gabriel Zucman and Emmanuel Saez are

[10] Scott Winship, "Whither The Bottom 90 Percent, Thomas Piketty?" April 17, 2014; www.forbes.com/sites/scottwinship/2014/04/17/whither-the-bottom-90-percent-thomas-piketty/.
[11] Chris Giles, "Piketty findings undercut by errors," Financial Times, May 23, 2014; www.ft.com/intl/cms/s/2/e1f343ca-e281-11e3-89fd-00144feabdc0.html#axzz34qcSbdft.

"more reliable" and should be used instead. Already, though, the new data also have been debunked, this time by economist Alan Reynolds.[12]

However, while the debate between economists, pundits, and policymakers goes on, in the larger public arena, I think Piketty has already won. Specifically, he has won because he has accomplished what appears to me to have been his goal: to set the issue of wealth inequality at the center of the public political debate. His American critics have become entangled in technical arguments about how concentrated wealth in America is and how best to measure that inequality. Piketty's progressive allies in America must be delighted, because they would like nothing better than to keep the political discussion focused on the "problem" of wealth inequality and what government supposedly can do to ameliorate it.

Piketty has performed a magic trick for the benefit of the progressive political movement here in the States. Just as a magician prevents people from seeing what is right in front of them by distracting them with misdirection, so "Cap21" is a red herring, distracting us from talking about the far more important economic and political questions—namely, what can we do to raise standards of living; what policies should Uncle Sam implement to facilitate economic growth; and most fundamentally of all, what is the proper role of government in economic matters?

---

[12] Alan Reynolds, "Why Piketty's Wealth Data Are Worthless," The Wall Street Journal, July 10, 2014, page A11.

Piketty devotes hundreds of pages to prove something that everyone already knows is true—that the distribution of wealth is very unequal. He insists on referring to this phenomenon as "inegalitarian." Piketty's choice of the adjective "inegalitarian," instead of the simpler "unequal," involves a semantic distinction rife with ideological implications. To state that wealth is unequally distributed is a statement of fact, devoid of normative content. To characterize it as inegalitarian, on the other hand, is to inject a value judgment. On dictionary.com, "egalitarian" is defined as "belief in the equality of all people, especially in political, economic, or social life."[13] The Merriam-Webster online dictionary definition is even more pointed: "aiming for equal wealth, status, etc., for all people."[14] The opposite of "egalitarian"— "inegalitarian"—denotes opposition to egalitarian beliefs; more specifically, an ideological inegalitarian believes that an unequal distribution of wealth is natural, that it is not inherently problematical or wrong, and consequently that government intervention to change the distribution of wealth is unnecessary and pointless.

**Inequality, economic and political**

Egalitarians inevitably bump into a stubborn reality: Human beings are and always have been unequal. The vitally important distinction that must be made is: Which of our differences are natural and which are artificial—that is, brought about by interferences with

---

[13] www.dictionary.reference.com/browse/egalitarian?s=t
[14] www.merriam-webster.com/dictionary/egalitarian

our natural differences? This determines whether the differences between us are just or unjust.

Few would say that it is unjust that you or I can't hit a baseball as well as Miguel Cabrera, play guitar like Jimi Hendrix, or compose music like Paul McCartney. We wouldn't consider it unfair that we don't have the inventiveness of Thomas Edison or the intuitive insight to make a scientific breakthrough that leads to a Nobel Prize. The individuals who excel in those areas have talents and skills that the rest of us simply don't have. That is nobody's fault. We were created to be different—unequal in our talents and abilities—whether you believe that the Creator is nature or God.

The same situation obtains in regard to entrepreneurial talent. Some individuals have a knack—the vision, courage, initiative, persistence, etc.—to organize factors of production in such a way as to create value for others. The talent of a Steve Jobs to make the Apple Corporation so immensely profitable is not a talent that most of us have. It is no more realistic to think it unfair that Steve Jobs had the entrepreneurial ability to build a company whose market value has risen to hundreds of billions of dollars than it would be to think it unfair that one cannot play basketball like LeBron James. However each of us employs our particular skills, talents, and knowledge to deliver economic value to others in the marketplace determines our income. Whatever we manage to save, either of our own income plus wealth given or bequeathed to us, is what determines how wealthy we are. It is the natural economic state of things that we reap what we sow. Nobody makes us poor or rich; we ourselves do that by our economic choices and performance.

## Freedom

What I have just described is the world of natural differences ("inequality," if you prefer) between individual human beings. However, there is an implicit precondition that must be present in order for our innate natural differences to blossom and enable each individual to realize the potential of his or her talents: people must be free if they are to be able to achieve their full potential in the social division of labor. Individual liberty is indispensable. When liberty is suppressed by force, whether that force is wielded by criminals or by government, the productive capacity of the amazing gifts and talents that individuals have may be stifled and repressed, and their value to society tragically lost.

For most of human history, it wasn't possible for most individuals with entrepreneurial genius to realize their potential. Their natural abilities were blunted by lack of opportunity imposed on them by repressive political power structures. Political power has been the means by which most of humankind's natural economic potential has been smothered and wasted. In fact, political power has been distributed very unequally. The political elite typically used their power to create and maintain an artificial economic inequality. That politically imposed economic inequality was not the inequality that would have resulted from the natural differences in individual skills and aptitudes. Instead, it was an unnatural inequality caused by the political elite having rigged the system so that they themselves owned, received, and controlled most of the society's wealth while the politically subservient masses shared an artificial approximate economic equality: They were wretchedly poor.

**Feudalism, mercantilism, and capitalism**

The political systems of feudalism and mercantilism that preceded the dawn of the Age of Capitalism in the 1700s were both rigid "status societies"—almost everyone died in the same social and economic class into which he or she had been born. It didn't matter if a feudal serf had an entrepreneurial genius with the potential to create vast amounts of wealth for thousands of people. In feudal society, the serf was not free to quit working on his lord's farm, nor did he have access to borrowing the capital needed to finance his entrepreneurial concept. His potential was doomed to lie fallow and remain unrealized. Similarly, under mercantilism, there must have been numerous individuals capable of becoming great wealth creators, capable of finding ways to supply a desired consumer good of higher quality yet for a lower price than existing suppliers, but they were not free to compete with the monarch's protected monopolists, the cronies of that era.

Both feudalism and mercantilism were systems in which the political elite rigged the economic game to enrich themselves while keeping the mass of people poor and disenfranchised. Under those politically unequal, repressive systems, human society lost an incalculable amount of valuable economic production. Tragically, and yes, unjustly, the natural gifts of millions of people never had a chance to flourish, but instead were suppressed by illiberal political systems. It shouldn't be surprising that wealth creation limped along lamely in a system where most people never had the freedom to use, develop and profit from their innate talents. As for the small minority holding the wealth and power, even those with entrepreneurial potential had little incentive to strive for greater productivity. They already were prospering from the rents they collected from the rigged system, and in many cases much of their energy was expended in managing and protecting their existing economic privileges.

The world has changed dramatically in the last few centuries. Enlightened thought led to breakthroughs in science, engineering, technology, commerce (i.e., free trade, mass production, and democratization of capital financing) and especially in the moral/ethical/political realm. The leaven of the Biblical message that each individual is equal in the eyes of God, and therefore each had "unalienable rights," broke up the old status societies—nowhere more radically than in the United States. These revolutionary ideas produced a quantum increase in individual liberty that (theoretically at least) gave each individual the opportunity to go as far as his or her natural talents would allow.

The American system was predicated on the principle that since all were equal in the eyes of God, all adult citizens, rich or poor, from the mansions of Manhattan to the wood cabins of Kentucky (think Abe Lincoln) were entitled to receive equal protection of their individual rights at the hands of law and government. Henry Ford, the son of a farmer in Michigan, never would have been free to build the largest automobile company in the world in a feudalist or mercantilist system; he needed the freedom of living in a system in which the government did no more for one member of society than another, in which markets were free rather than rigged by a political elite.

The American ideal of law and government rendering impartial justice to unequally talented and endowed individuals was eloquently articulated by our seventh president, Andrew Jackson:

> Distinctions in society will always exist under every just government. Equality of talents, of education, or of wealth cannot be produced by human institutions. In the full enjoyment of the gifts of Heaven and the fruits of superior industry, economy, and virtue, every many is equally entitled to protection by law; but when the laws undertake to add to these natural and just advantages artificial distinctions, to grant titles, gratuities and exclusive privileges, to make the rich richer and the potent more powerful, the humble members of society—the farmers, mechanics and laborers—who have neither the time nor the means of securing like favors to themselves, have

a right to complain of the injustice of
their Government.[15]

The most obvious economic result of the American
system of "equality before the law" is that the United
States quickly became the wealthiest country in the
world, even before the end of the 19th century. More
wealth has been created here than anywhere else.
Upward social mobility has been unprecedented. More
and more Americans have become millionaires. The
masses of middle-income Americans enjoy a level of
affluence unimaginable just a few generations ago.
Even those officially categorized as poor own
amenities[16] (e.g., cars, refrigerators, televisions, etc.)
that are the stuff of dreams for billions who live abroad.

Now, let us be very clear about what the American ideal
of equality before the law does and does not do: When
practiced more consistently than it is today, the
principle of equality before the law gets rid of political
inequality wherein a self-perpetuating elite subjugates
most of the population to permanent second-class status.
It does not, however, eliminate economic inequality.
Instead, it changes its character by making the
attainment of wealth dependent upon merit rather than
status, that is, by elevating to the economic elite those
who do the best job of supplying the needs and wants of
others in a competitive marketplace. This stands in stark
contrast to a system with an entrenched political elite

---

[15] Andrew Jackson in James D. Richardson, ed., A
Compilation of the Messages and Papers of the Presidents;
Bureau of National Literarture and Art; 1910; 2:1153.
[16] www.antolin-
davies.com/conventionalwisdom/uspoverty.pdf.

whose wealth comes from rigging the system to enrich themselves at the expense of others.

The fortunes, both large and small, that successful entrepreneurs make in a capitalist system are the key to our rising standards of living. Rather than resent such fortunes, we should applaud and welcome them. The fact is that the more millionaires[17] there are in a capitalist society, the better conditions are for non-millionaires. That is because each fortune signifies more wealth created for others, and also because the more millionaires there are, the more capital there is to finance additional entrepreneurial wealth-creating endeavors. More capital leads to more business creation, and more businesses in existence means more competition, hence higher wages and higher standards of living for workers.

Critics grumble about large fortunes, but lose sight of the social benefits of those fortunes. The social benefits are twofold: First, the largest entrepreneurial fortunes always have been earned via mass production, i.e., production that supplies goods and services to the masses, raising their standard of living. Second, every dollar of profit is the reflection of at least a dollar of value that has been created for the common man, because as long as the transactions between consumer and supplier are voluntary, they will happen only when they are based on mutual gain. This principle of positive-sum exchanges, by the way, is one of the first

---

[17] Mark W. Hendrickson, "Millionaires in America," The Center for Vision & Values, April 29, 2011; www.visionandvalues.org/2011/04/millionaires-in-america/

laws of capitalism, far more important that the arid arithmetical formula that Piketty highlights in "Cap21."

One socially transforming effect of free-market systems based on equality before the law is that, by doing away with political elites, such systems generate rapid and unpredictable changes in the composition of the economic elite. The *nouveaux riches* frequently replace the "old money" at the top of the economic heap. From the richest to the poorest member of a capitalist society, individuals frequently leap-frog those ahead of them on the economic ladder. The grandchildren (sometimes even the children) of those at the top today are likely to be unknown several decades hence. There is no established, hereditary economic elite in the absence of a political elite.

The bottom line for capitalism is this: It will raise standards of living for the masses far more effectively than feudalism and mercantilism, and for that matter, socialism. As is the case under those other economic systems, wealth will be distributed unequally, but only under capitalism is the distribution of wealth determined not on the basis of political connections, but on the meritocratic and beneficent principle of the most wealth going to those who have created the most wealth for others.

### Piketty's egalitarianism

The capitalist system, based on equality before the law, is inegalitarian by definition. Piketty and his fellow progressives are ideological "egalitarians"—they believe that an unequal distribution of wealth and inequality of living standards are inherently unjust. Indeed, Piketty repeatedly invokes "social justice"—the doctrine that a more just social order is one in which wealth is distributed more "fairly," i.e., equally, than it currently is (See pages 26, 96, 234).

An egalitarian society, in which the goal is a more equal distribution of wealth, can only be attained if government and laws treat individuals unequally or differently—often to a very radical extent. Egalitarianism rejects the American principle of equality before the law with everyone having equal freedom to earn and accumulate however much wealth they lawfully and honestly can. Instead, the egalitarian creed aims for equality of condition. Egalitarians believe that all citizens have an equal right to have certain things, rather than just have the freedom to try to obtain those things—in Karl Marx's words—"from each according to his ability to each according to his need."

The equality of condition that egalitarians espouse is explicit in "Cap21." Piketty writes, "the professed equality of rights of all citizens contrasts sharply with the very real inequality of living conditions" (page 422). The right of citizens to be supplied with certain economic goods, regardless of whether they have rendered any economic service to others, is also explicit: "Modern redistribution, as exemplified by the social states constructed by the wealthy countries in the twentieth century, is based on a set of fundamental social rights: to education, health, and retirement" (page 481).

Obviously, the only way that government can provide costly economic goods such as education and healthcare is to appropriate the wealth needed to pay for those goods from other citizens—in other words, to redistribute wealth. Such a system must negate the right of some citizens to keep their property in the name of fulfilling the supposed rights of other citizens to have that property.

Although Piketty unequivocally favors strong government action to distribute wealth more equally, he occasionally lapses into inconsistent statements about inequality that undermine his contention that we are confronted with a menacing problem that requires drastic action. He writes, "there is no doubt that inequality of wealth today stands significantly below its level of a century ago" (page 346, supported by charts corroborating this statement for France, Britain, and Sweden on pages 340, 344, & 345). He also reports that "the world seems to have entered a phase in which rich and poor countries are converging in income" (page 67).[18] This convergence is good news, because since the rich countries clearly aren't regressing, convergence can only mean that many countries are climbing out of their age-old poverty.

---

[18] Elsewhere (p. 572) Piketty contradicts the two statements just quoted, when he writes about "the unlimited growth of global inequality, which is currently increasing at a rate that cannot be sustained..."

## Inegalitarian success stories

The key point to recognize is that today's economically vibrant countries have not adopted egalitarian policies. To varying extents, they have strengthened property rights and the rule of law while reducing bureaucratic restraints and burdens. They have unleashed entrepreneurs and welcomed profit-making enterprises. By welcoming capital rather than trying to find ways to reduce it, and by placing economic growth higher in importance than the equal distribution of wealth, the economic improvements in certain countries have been meteoric: Chile's per capita GDP has risen from $550 in 1960 to $15,300 in 2012; China's has risen from $92 to $6,078 during that same period; while Singapore's has exploded from $395 to $53,516 according to the IMF's April 2014 database.[19]

The case of China deserves special attention, because it is a country run by an entrenched political elite that is rapidly becoming fabulously wealthy. The country nevertheless is experiencing amazing growth because, rather than suppress the economic aspirations of the masses the way the political elites of feudalism and mercantilism did, the Chinese leaders are doing everything they can to get the non-elite to prosper, too, and they are doing much to encourage and support profit-making enterprises.

---

[19]

www.wikipedia.org/wiki/List_of_countries_by_past_and_future_GDP_(nominal)_per_capita

The result of the rapid economic growth in China is that there is considerable inequality there. Millionaires[20] and billionaires[21] have been proliferating, but the real story is the concurrent dramatic increase in standards of living enjoyed by a majority of the country's population. As recently as 2000, only 4 percent of urban households in China were middle class; by 2012, that share soared to 68 percent.[22] China has treated capital like a friend and benefactor, not a menace or enemy. As measured by Foreign Direct Investment (an imperfect but helpful proxy for capital flows) statistics gathered by the World Bank, FDI in China increased from $38.4 billion in 2000 to $253.5 billion in 2012.[23] The lesson is plain: the more capital, the greater the improvement in standards of living. The rising economic prosperity of China, like the earlier rise of the US, illustrates the validity of a principle articulated by Ludwig von Mises—what could be called the first rule of capitalism as applied to economic growth: *A country becomes*

---

[20] Frederik Balfour, "China's Millionaires Leap Past 1 Million on Growth, Savings," Bloomberg.com, June1, 2011; www.bloomberg.com/news/2011-05-31/china-s-millionaires-jump-past-one-million-on-savings-growth.html.
[21] Malcolm Moore, "China's billionaires double in number," The Telegraph, September 7, 2011; www.telegraph.co.uk/news/worldnews/asia/china/8746445/Chinas-billionaires-double-in-number.html.
[22] www.china.org.cn/business/2014-03/20/content_31858451.htm
[23]
http://www.worldbank.org/indicator/BX.KLT.DINV.CD.W. We have been unable to find a workable URL to access these data, even though both the World Bank and UN publish them online. If you google "FDI in China World Bank data," the first link that comes up should say "data.worldbank.org..." and lead you to the data.

*more prosperous in proportion to the rise in the invested capital per unit of its population.*[24]

### The high cost of egalitarianism – political, social, ethical and economic consequences

We in America should think very carefully of the price we would pay if we adopted Piketty's egalitarian principles. There are considerable tradeoffs that would have to be made to make the distribution of wealth more equal.

Politically, the only feasible way to make the distribution of wealth more equal would be for government to treat citizens unequally before the law. The government would do even more than it now does to take more wealth from certain citizens and give more wealth to certain other citizens. Egalitarianism exalts equality of wealth as a higher value than the inegalitarian, American value of equality of opportunity. Piketty and the progressives want to taking us in a retrograde direction—back to a system run by a political elite (in the name of democracy, of course). In fact, the egalitarian road leads to socialism. The actual practice of socialism, *contra* the idealistic rhetoric, is government by an elite that makes all the key economic decisions about who produces what and who gets what. Socialism retards the economic progress of the masses

---

[24] Ludwig von Mises, Economic Policy, South Bend IN: Regnery Gateway, 1979, p. 14; www.mises.org/document/994/Economic-Policy-Thoughts-for-Today-and-Tomorrow

33

and picks economic winners and losers, just like feudalism and mercantilism did.

Socially, egalitarian policies would increase societal tensions and promote class conflict. In a free market, where transactions are voluntary and mutually agreed upon, therefore positive sum, certain people may not particularly like other people, but they have an incentive to peacefully cooperate with them. In a system in which some individuals, via the government, have power to take from other individuals, there is more of a reason to perceive those others as enemies instead of allies. Political inequality arrays neighbor against neighbor, thereby undermining social harmony and sowing the seeds of class conflict. Forced equality of wealth would short-circuit the vibrant social mobility that characterizes a free market system. Radical cries about revolutionary class warfare never gained popularity in America because so many Americans rose so quickly into higher economic strata that class lines never had time to congeal. Apparently, what Piketty found objectionable about the rigid economic order described in the novels of Austen and Balzac was not the politically imposed social rigidity per se, but the fact that the rigidity locked people into economic differences rather than economic sameness.

Ethically, there is something perverse about singling out society's economic benefactors for persecution rather than commendation. In a free market, one reaps what one sows, not what someone else sows. That hardly seems unjust. To profit in a free market, one has to do something to help others economically. Should government impose discriminatory punishments against those who do the most economic good for others?

Economically, a government-imposed equal distribution of wealth inevitably makes society overall poorer.[25] When government taxes capital, as Piketty urges in "Cap21," government immediately spends it and it is gone, thereby leaving less capital to invest in market-based, wealth-producing activities. This slows economic growth, and slow economic growth hurts the poor most of all. Redistribution of wealth alters the incentives that individuals face, and radical redistribution erodes the incentive to put forth one's best effort to produce wealth—the productive citizen, because he no longer receives large rewards for his efforts, and the unproductive citizen, since he knows that he'll be taken care of regardless of how little he works. Lyndon Johnson's "War on Poverty," launched in the 1960s, had the unintended consequence of interrupting the long-term secular trend toward lower poverty rates in the U.S. Indeed, Charles Murray's landmark 1984 book, "Losing Ground," showed conclusively that once the federal government declared war on poverty, the long-term historical trend toward lower poverty rates was aborted and the rate of poverty

---

[25] A July 4, 2014 working paper by economists Allan Meltzer and Scott Richard, entitled, "A Rational Theory of the Growth of Government and the Distribution of Income" comes to the conclusion that "using redistribution to ameliorate income inequality is not only ineffective, but worsens the problem that policy makers seek to cure." Diana Furchtgott-Roth, "Piketty's cure for income inequality hurts the poor," MarketWatch.com, July 10, 2014; http://www.marketwatch.com/story/pikettys-cure-for-income-inequality-hurts-the-poor-2014-07-10

more or less leveled off. Here we are five decades and trillions of dollars farther along with no real progress at reducing the poverty rate.

### Depressions better than booms?

Piketty looks favorably on the data showing a reduction in wealth inequality during the Great Depression (page 275), although he undoubtedly wishes that the change had happened without the poor bearing the brunt of the contraction and millions of formerly employed people being reduced to begging and soup kitchens. Conversely, Piketty laments the increased growth in capital's share of income (i.e., increased wealth inequality) during the Reagan years (page 42), even though the poverty rate fell by one-sixth in only five years once Reagan's policies took hold,[26] with African-Americans in particular registering sizable, rapid economic gains during the Reagan years.[27] These two passages (pages 275 and 42) are troublesome for two reasons: 1) they evince such an intense antipathy for wealthy individuals that Piketty appears to favor depressions to boom times, and 2) they are inconsistent with his own statements asserting that fast growth facilitates rather than impedes an equalization of wealth

---

[26] Peter Ferrara, "Reaganomics Vs. Obamanomics: Facts And Figures," Forbes.com May 5, 2011; www.forbes.com/sites/peterferrara/2011/05/05/reaganomics-vs-obamanomics-facts-and-figures/.

[27] Paul Kengor, "10 years after Reagan's death: How does Obama's record compare to Reagan's?" FoxNews.com, June 5, 2014; www.foxnews.com/opinion/2014/06/05/10-years-after-ronald-reagans-death-how-does-reagans-record-compare-to-obamas/.

(see "Errors of omission," #2, for a more detailed discussion).

### The choice – reduce inequality or reduce poverty?

Piketty and the other egalitarians have made a grim choice: In a world in which economic growth—the production of wealth—is the antidote for poverty, they believe that it is more important for government to reduce the unequal distribution of wealth through forced redistribution than it is to reduce poverty. Like it or not, measures designed to reduce inequality will slow growth and hinder progress against poverty. Egalitarians seem oblivious to the truth that the greatest progress against poverty is made in "inegalitarian" systems. They reject a polity in which total wealth increases faster and reaches more people, but a relatively small number of individuals get a lot richer while most people's standard of living improves more modestly.

Piketty tells us that these major decisions will be made democratically, and he is correct. If we choose his egalitarian path, we will achieve something far different from the stated utopian goal of a just, blissful, harmonious equality. A government dedicated to implementing egalitarian policies will necessarily be a more powerful government. It would produce a stratified society divided into two major classes—a political ruling elite and everyone else beneath them. Such a government not only would be able to redistribute wealth more radically than it does today, but may use its expanded powers to negatively impact our lives in ways that supporters of economic equality haven't even considered. Greater economic equality would be bought at the price of slower economic growth, hence less progress against poverty, and less individual liberty

We Americans were facing this choice even before "Cap21" appeared. We can now thank Thomas Piketty for making us think more deeply about the kind of government we want to have in the 21$^{st}$ century and beyond.

# Part Two:
# A detailed
# examination

**Dropping a bomb on the first law of capitalism after enchanting the reader**

Let's proceed now to a detailed examination of "Cap21." I may be wrong, but it seems that Piketty's inclusion of the works of two popular novelists of a bygone ear—Jane Austen and Honoré de Balzac—has two purposes. Beyond the glimpses of a bygone era, I think his intent is to win over his readers (particularly those who aren't trained in economics) by using literature, instead of cold and possibly intimidating charts and tables, to establish rapport with his readers. He comes across as a reasonable, pleasant, easy-going guy, an amiable man and a sincere scholar—the antithesis of a bomb-throwing radical. In fact, I found myself wanting to have lunch with him.

Then, after 50 (actually, 51) pages of disarming prose, "BAM!" Like the proverbial "bolt out of the blue," Piketty suddenly detonates a veritable bomb: On page 52, he proclaims that "the first fundamental law of capitalism" is a formula—"the share of income from capital in national income" is equal to "the rate of return on capital" times "the capital/income ratio."

This assertion is, to put it bluntly, absurd. The objection here is not to the accounting formula itself, but to the presumptuous attempt to redefine capitalism in the author's own esoteric way. I have been an economist longer than Piketty; I have read the writings of the great economic exponents of capitalism from Adam Smith through John Stuart Mill, Carl Menger, Ludwig von Mises, and on through Milton Friedman, Hans Sennholz, Arthur Laffer, et al., and this is the first time I have ever encountered Piketty's claim that an accounting formula comprises "the first fundamental law of capitalism." It is rather unfair for someone who disdains capitalism as much as Piketty does (on page 350, he writes about putting "the evil genie of capitalism…back into its bottle") to be the one to redefine it. This is no more fair than relying on a militant Iranian ayatollah for an accurate definition of Judaism.

The actual first law, or principle, of capitalism is that the economic means of production are privately owned and controlled, and that government exists to act as an impartial economic referee, not to pick winners and losers or to participate as a competing player in the economic affairs of a country.[28] A more accurate title for Piketty's book would be "How to Suppress Capitalism in the 21st Century."

If you don't understand Piketty's formula, don't worry about it. He asserts it to lay a foundation for his principal thesis—namely, that the inexorable trend of free-market capitalism is for the rich to get richer at a faster rate than the poor and middle class; that the resulting increased concentration of wealth will lead to unstable, untenable conditions that will culminate in unspecified disasters; therefore, government should intervene—specifically, to redistribute wealth via a global tax on accumulated wealth. Let's now take a

---

[28] See my six-part series defining "Capital, Capitalists and Capitalism"; www.frontpagemag.com/2013/mark-hendrickson/capital-capitalists-and-capitalism-part-vi/ which has links to the other five parts.

more detailed look at some other problematical content from "Cap21."

**Errors of commission - dubious economics and other problematical statements**

When it comes to identifying economic errors and fallacies, one must acknowledge that the economics profession has strong disagreements about which concepts and theories are true or valid. I will point out what I perceive as errors in "Cap21," and you decide if you agree.

1) Ignoring incentives

"We may assume that accounting for tax avoidance and evasion would increase the levels of inequality derived from tax returns by similar proportions in different periods and would therefore not substantially modify the time trends and evolutions I have identified" (page 282). This statement ignores the crucial role that incentives play in human action, and the corresponding fact that individual human beings respond differently to different incentives. When tax rates are high, the incentive to avoid or evade taxes is higher, and when tax rates are low, the same incentives are much diminished; thus, since high-income earners face higher tax rates than lower-income earners, the incentives they face are different, and changes in income reported will not remain in "similar proportions in different periods."

## 2) Clinging to the labor theory of value

Piketty writes as if he is still at least partially under the influence of the labor theory of value—the now-defunct 19$^{th}$-century belief that all value is produced by labor and therefore the entrepreneur's profits and the capitalist's returns are unjustified. The labor theory, found in the writings of the classical economists Adam Smith and David Ricardo (although Ricardo listed numerous exceptions), was elevated to an absolute first principle by a later writer, Karl Marx. In the late 1800s, the Austrian economist Eugen von Böhm-Bawerk[29] famously demolished and buried the labor theory to the satisfaction of all except hardcore revolutionary ideologues. Nevertheless, the ghostly shadow of the labor theory darkens the pages of "Cap21" periodically.

For example, Piketty resents "the spectacular enrichment of octogenarians [that] cannot be explained by income from labor or entrepreneurial activity" (page 394). He finds it distasteful that large fortunes may grow "regardless of whether the owner of the fortune works or not" (page 439). "Is it useful and just," he asks, "for the owners of capital [to receive a return on capital] even if they contribute no new work?" (page 215)

Because he bristles at wealth not produced directly by a person's own labor, Piketty disdains inherited fortunes, condescendingly commenting, "Obviously wealth is not just a matter of merit" (page 441). Elsewhere, he

---

[29] "Eugen von Böhm-Bawerk, Karl Marx and the Close of His System," 1986; available from The Mises Institute, https://mises.org/books/karlmarx.pdf.

affirms his "belief in a society in which inequality [of wealth] is based more on merit and effort ["effort" being a synonym of "labor"] than on kinship and rents" (page 422)—i.e. inherited wealth and accumulated capital. Incidentally, Piketty misuses the pejorative term "rents" when he equates it to "accumulated wealth."

Surely Piketty must realize that wealth is not determined by effort, for he must know academic colleagues who have worked as hard as he has without receiving the extra income that Piketty is now receiving from having written a best-selling book. Alas, Piketty seems oblivious to the elementary economic principle that one earns wealth in capitalism by creating value for others, and not by how much effort one expends.

Hobbled by not having entirely shaken off the labor theory of value, Piketty tends to view value as objective rather than subjective. Value, like beauty, is in the eye of the beholder, and thus differs from person to person or, indeed, the same person at different times. In criticizing the "increased pay at the very top end of the distribution" (e.g., multimillion-dollar pay packages for CEOs of American corporations), Piketty imagines that there is no appreciable difference between the CEO and thousands of other workers "regardless of what criteria we use: years of education, selectivity of educational institution, or professional experience"—i.e., in "'objective' measures of skill and productivity" (page 314). What eludes him is that boards of directors often select top executives for reasons that are subjective, not objective. Perhaps they see someone as a rare visionary, maybe a charismatic leader with a knack for motivating the corporate team—who knows? The key point to understand, both in terms of economic theory and actual events, is that people often are hired for intangibles that can't be quantified objectively. I don't say this to be mean, but Piketty's understanding of value is antiquated. It is based on a fallacy that much of the economics profession left behind in the 1870s, when Carl Menger articulated the subjective theory of value.[30]

3) Static analysis

One of the most common errors in economic analysis is to neglect to account for changes that happen over time. Economic life is a motion picture, not a photograph. Things change. Yet, in "Cap21," Piketty employs a static analysis when constructing hypothetical examples about long-term inequality of incomes. On page 256, he compares "a person who all his or her life earns 7,000 euros a month rather than 4,000," and on page 420, he presents a hypothetical case of someone earning approximately the minimum wage "over the course of a fifty-year career (including retirement)." In both cases, he completely ignores the fact that, in real life in a capitalist society, as opposed to an economist's theories, individuals' incomes fluctuate considerably over the course of a lifetime.

4) Misdiagnosing the financial crisis of 2008-09

In a section titled "Did the Increase of Inequality In the United States Cause the Financial Crisis?" Piketty

---

[30] Thomas W. Hazlett, "Carl Menger: Ivory Tower Iconoclast," *The Freeman*, May 1, 1977; www.fee.org/the_freeman/detail/carl-menger-ivory-tower-iconoclast.

writes, "In my view, there is absolutely no doubt that the increase in inequality in the United States contributed to the nation's financial instability." (page 297) To his credit, by using the phrase "In my view…." Piketty tacitly admits that he is offering nothing more than an opinion. The opinion, however, does not withstand scrutiny.

In the first place, pronounced wealth inequality has been a constant throughout American history, whereas severe economic crises erupt only occasionally. Secondly and more importantly, what presumably motivates egalitarians is the goal of the non-rich becoming more prosperous (a worthy goal that I share). Here's where Piketty's opinion falls apart: The data show that Americans' prosperity, as shown by median incomes[31] and median net worth,[32] was trending higher before the financial crisis, but tumbled badly after it.[33] The sequence was this: Rising median incomes and net worth did not precede, hence could not have caused, the crisis, but in the aftermath of the crisis, median incomes and net worth declined while the poverty rate rose from 12.5 to 14.3 percent.[34] For anyone to imply that rising prosperity triggered the crisis gives rise to an illogical

31
en.wikipedia.org/wiki/Personal_income_in_the_United_State
s#mediaviewer/File:Per_capita_US_income.png
[32] blogs.reuters.com/felix-salmon/2012/06/12/chart-of-the-day-median-net-worth-1962-2010/
[33] Mark Hendrickson, "Obama's War on the Middle Class," May 24, 2013; www.frontpagemag.com/2013/mark-hendrickson/obamas-war-on-the-middle-class/.
[34] "The President of Inequality," *The Wall Street Journal*, October 3, 2014, p. A12.

conundrum: that economic progress reduces prosperity and increases poverty—a self-evident absurdity.

Given the harmful impact of the crisis on the very people for whom Piketty professes concern, it is peculiar that he didn't analyze the causes of the devastating crisis more carefully. He simply ignored the plethora of major policy mistakes that caused the financial crisis and delayed the subsequent recovery[35]: Federal regulators with grandiose plans of social engineering who colluded with the government-sponsored agencies Fannie Mae and Freddie Mac to distort and ultimately devastate the housing and financial markets; central bankers chronically warping credit markets and tampering with interest rates; clueless congressmen and presidents whose reflex response is to throw more money at problems (e.g., the Bush Administration's panicky Wall Street bailout and the Obama administrations non-stimulating "stimulus plan")—these are the culprits who misallocated trillions of dollars of assets and caused the crisis. (Piketty, it turns out, has a major blind spot in regard to government-caused economic mischief: See section "Errors of Omission.")

5) An exaggerated faith in education

Several times in "Cap21," Piketty singles out education as "the best way to reduce inequalities with respect to labor." Furthermore, the best policy "to increase the

---

[35] See, for example, Thomas E. Woods, Jr., "Meltdown," Washington, DC: Regnery Publishing, Inc., 2009 and John A. Allison, "The Financial Crisis and the Free Market Cure," New York: McGraw Hill, 2013.

average productivity of the labor force and the overall growth of the economy is surely to invest in education" (pages 306-7). On the positive side, this is one of the few places in "Cap21" where Piketty attempts to articulate a pro-growth policy. And he is correct, at least, in a narrower sense than what he means: Unless there is a radical improvement in many failed public schools, particularly in our inner cities, the prospects for upward economic mobility for the kids stuck there will be relatively limited.

However, simply spending more money on education, as Piketty advocates (e.g., page 71), easily can turn out to be money wasted. According to the Bureau of Labor Statistics, in October 2013, 65.9 percent of 2013 high school graduates were enrolled in higher education,[36] yet the same federal agency reported (2012 data) that only "about one-third of jobs were in occupations that typically require postsecondary education for entry."[37] Perhaps that is why more than half of those holding bachelor's degrees in recent years have found themselves either underemployed or unemployed.[38]

Certainly, there must be better ways to increase opportunities for the best and brightest youth to pursue a post-secondary education if they so desire, but as any of us who currently teach in college classrooms here in the States can attest, there are too many pupils already

---

[36] www.bls.gov/news.release/hsgec.nro.htm.
[37] www.bls.gov/emp/ep-edtrain_outlook.pdf.
[38] (AP) "Half of new graduates are jobless of underemployed," April 23, 2012;
www.usatoday30.usatoday.com/news/nation/story/2012-04-22/college-grads-jobless/54473426/1.

enrolled who either aren't ready or able to do college-level work satisfactorily. Simply increasing enrollments isn't the answer, because people are not fungible; that is, you cannot put people into college classrooms and glibly assume that they will be turned into something they are not. Given the current job market, one can make a convincing case that the number of post-secondary students should decrease rather than increase.[39]

6) The inheritance bogeyman

To strengthen his case for high tax rates on inheritances, Piketty depicts inheritances as some sort of economic monster: "the past tends to devour the future: wealth originating in the past automatically grows more rapidly [than newer wealth]. Almost inevitably, this tends to give lasting, disproportionate importance to inequalities created in the past, and therefore to inheritance" (page 378). Apart from being a totally unproven assertion, this clearly isn't how the world works. If it were, then the Astors, Rockefellers, Fords, and DuPonts would still be at the top of the financial heap, and not people like Bill Gates, Warren Buffett, and Mark Zuckerberg.

---

[39] Mark Hendrickson, "Myth-busting 101: Uncomfortable Truths Your College Won't Tell You – Parts I and II, Forbes.com, August 16 & 19, 2012; www.forbes.com/sites/markhendrickson/2012/08/19/myth busting-101-uncomfortable-truths-your-college-wont-tell-you-part-ii/.

49

7) Taxes as wealth creators?

In a discussion about the percentage of national income taken by taxes in various parts of the world (generally, in recent decades, 10-15 percent in South Asia and sub-Saharan Africa, 15-20 percent in Latin America, North Africa, and China, and 30-40 percent in the most of the world's prosperous countries), Piketty treads on thin ice by asserting, "In all the developed countries in the world today, building a fiscal and social state has been an essential part of the process of modernization and economic development" (page 491). Here he clearly puts the cart before the horse. The rich countries aren't rich because their governments have taxed their citizens more than the governments in poor countries have; rather, the taxpayers in richer countries are able to afford higher taxes precisely because they already are wealthier than poor countries. Piketty's line of reasoning implies that poor countries can boost their economic development by raising taxes. In reality, a tax burden of "only" 10-15 percent feels heavy to poor people, and if the governments of poor countries were to raise taxes, those higher taxes would crush the poor, making them even poorer.

8) Beneficent and just inflation?

For one who professes a great concern for justice, Piketty adopts a bewildering view of inflation: "one argument in favor of inflation [is that it] primarily penalizes people who do not know what to do with their money, namely, those who have kept too much cash in their bank account or stuffed into their mattresses...Better still, it spares those who are in debt"

50

(page 546). Thus, Piketty commends inflation both for punishing savers—including many middle-class citizens who are trying to save for a comfortable retirement—and for bailing out debtors–citizens who in many cases have spent beyond their means. Why Piketty favors a practice that punishes the prudent while rewarding the imprudent makes neither economic nor ethical sense to me.

9) Errors of historical fact

Perhaps most salient of the dubious statements and outright errors contained in "Cap21" are several major errors of fact in Piketty's retelling of American history:

a) He repeats the common error, "The traditional doctrine of 'laissez faire,' or nonintervention by the state in the economy, to which all countries adhered in the nineteenth century and to a large extent until nearly 1930s, was durably discredited" (page 136) by the Great Depression. The historical fact is that, unlike the Depression of 1920-21, to which the federal policy response was truly of the laissez-faire variety (first Harding, then Coolidge, slashed government spending and significantly reduced federal tax rates,[40] giving rise to the fantastic economic boom of the 1920s), President Hoover, a decade later, spurned the laissez-faire philosophy and intervened massively in a failed attempt to end the depression. In fact, the combined Hoover-

---

[40] Mark Hendrickson, "Yo-Yo Economics?" April 26, 2012; www.forbes.com/sites/markhendrickson/2012/04/26/yo-yo-economics/.

Roosevelt interventions were what spawned the Great Depression.[41] So extensive were Hoover's interventions that Roosevelt campaigned against him in 1932, complaining of extravagant federal spending and irresponsible deficit spending. Vice presidential candidate John Nance Garner even accused Hoover of socialism.[42] Years later, Rexford G. Tugwell, an influential member of FDR's brain trust, attested, "We didn't admit it at the time, but practically the whole New Deal was extrapolated from programs that Hoover started."[43]

b) When presenting a cursory history of the U.S.'s graduated income tax, Piketty repeatedly bungles the rates and dates. The top income tax rate under Hoover was not "only 25 percent," (page 473) but 63 percent. This increase happened under Hoover in 1932 (retroactive to January 1), not under FDR in 1933, as Piketty erroneously states on page 507. Furthermore, the top rate did not "stabilize at around 90 percent until the mid-1960s" before falling to "70 percent in the early 1980s" (page 507). President Kennedy secured passage of legislation that reduced the top rate to 70 percent by 1965, and

[41] Lawrence W. Reed, "Great Myths of the Great Depression"; The Freeman, August 1998; www.fee.org/library/detail/great-myths-of-the-great-depression-pdf-and-audio.
[42] Cf. "FDR's Disputed Legacy," Time, February 1, 1982, p. 23.
[43] Paul Johnson, "A History of the American People" (New York: HarperCollins Publishers, 1997), page 741.

President Reagan further reduced it to 50 percent in the early 1980s, then to 28 percent in 1986.

c) Piketty also gets his dates and rates wrong when discussing the federal minimum wage. He declares that the minimum wage "remained stuck at $3.25" (page 309) under George H.W. Bush, when in fact Bush signed legislation increasing it to $3.80 in 1990 and $4.25 in 1991. Instead of remaining frozen at Clinton-era levels "under George W. Bush before being increased several times by Barack Obama," as Piketty asserts, the facts are that the younger Bush signed legislation raising the minimum wage by 41 percent over three years, from $5.15 to $7.25, while Obama has yet to sign into law an increase of the minimum wage.

10) Distorting reality

In a strange hypothetical example, Piketty speculates that for those already wealthy to accumulate additional wealth equal to dozens of years of national income (a far greater accumulation of wealth than ever has existed), it "might require several generations to forgo consumption" (page 564). This is an off-the-wall scenario. In reality, no generation is capable of forgoing consumption—they would die. Besides, how are capitalists ever going to earn a return on capital if nobody consumes the product of their capital?

The bizarreness of this statement is compounded in the accompanying endnote, in which, after stating the

53

economic truth, "Capital and labor work hand in hand," he goes on to say that "this depends on institutions such as taxes and public ownership" (page 652). He appears to be saying that free markets cannot function on their own with private ownership—a self-evident absurdity when we recall that, by definition, free markets are based on private property and there are abundant examples proving that free markets flourish more vigorously than government-planned markets ever have (e.g., 19th century USA, 21st century Singapore).

**Credit for stating some important economic truths**

Before I continue with my criticisms of "Cap21," I offer you a brief interlude: Here let me acknowledge some of the sound economic statements Piketty includes in his text. Certainly, "Cap21," like most economic treatises, is a case of "tares and wheat"—a mixed bag. As stated earlier, Piketty has irritated some of his friends on the left by making concessions to economic and capitalist reality instead of writing undiluted hardcore ideological dogma. Here are several examples of commendable economic wisdom in "Cap21": "Obviously, raising the minimum wage cannot continue indefinitely: as the minimum wage increases, the negative effects on the level of employment eventually win out" (page 313) and, "If capital plays a useful role in the process of production, it is natural that it should be paid" (page 423). He is correct in his observation that "the redistribution induced by inflation is mainly to the detriment of the least wealthy and to the benefit of the wealthiest" (page 455) Bravo! Also, although he strongly believes that the government should have the lead role in providing pensions, this "does not mean that it would not be wise to encourage people of more modest means to accumulate nest eggs of their own" (page 490). Similarly, although central banks play a crucial role in Piketty's overall scheme, he recognizes that there are limits to their powers, writing, "indeed, it would be astonishing if central banks could simply by the stroke of a pen increase the capital of their nation or the world" (page 550). These are all clear statements of economic wisdom. I just wish there had been more of them. Unfortunately, too many needed explanations were omitted entirely from "Cap21." I'll address the most glaring omissions next.

**Errors of omission – Piketty's blind spots**

Piketty's biases lead him to ignore or barely mention with a passing reference certain topics that are essential aspects of the issues he raises. There are three issues conspicuously absent from "Cap21"—government spending, economic growth, and the indispensable role of capital in raising standards of living.

1) Government spending

Piketty shares this reviewer's aversion to public debt. He explicitly declares, "At the moment, the rich countries of the world are enmeshed in a seemingly interminable debt crisis" (page 540). Also: "I have no particular liking for public debt...[because] debt often becomes a backhanded form of redistribution of wealth from the poor to the rich." (page 566). He complains, "we currently spend far more in interest on the debt than we invest in higher education," then follows with a call for action: "the debt must be reduced as quickly as possible" because "debt weighs very heavily on our public finances" (page 567). Despite his concerns about debt, nowhere within "Cap21"'s nearly 600 pages of text does Piketty recommend the most obvious way to get the debt problem under control—i.e., by reducing government expenditures. On the contrary, he explicitly opposes laws or constitutions that would cap government spending (page 566).

There simply is no room in Piketty's worldview to question the legitimacy, wisdom, justice, or efficacy of government spending. He simply accepts it *a priori* as good and right. Thus, in answering his own question, "How can a public debt as large as today's European debt be significantly reduced?" he states, "There are three main methods, which can be combined in various proportions: taxes on capital, inflation, and austerity. An exceptional tax on private capital is the most just and efficient solution. Failing that, inflation can play a useful role: historically, that is how most large public debts have been dealt with. The worst solution in terms of both justice and efficiency is a prolonged dose of austerity—yet that is the course Europe is currently following" (page 541).

The word "austerity" in this context is misleading.[44] It is a favorite buzzword invoked by those who favor more government spending, higher taxes, and a greater

44 Mark W. Hendrickson, "Understanding 'Austerity,'" The Center for Vision & Values, August 20, 2010; www.visionandvalues.org/2010/08/understanding-austerity/.

transfer of wealth from the private to the public sector. What most progressives call "austerity" is simply the fiscally sound practice of a government refraining from spending in excess of its revenues (which, by the way, most European governments have not been doing,[45] contrary to Piketty's assertion). When Mr. Smith's income is $50,000 after-tax for a year, and he has no savings to tap into, we wouldn't call it "austerity" if Mr. Smith refrained from spending more than $50,000, but simply common sense. Yet Piketty asserts that government living within its budget violates both justice and efficiency. Citing "efficiency" seems almost Orwellian—the notion that it is more efficient for government to spend in excess of its revenues rather than to balance its revenues with its expenditures turns the concept of efficiency on its head.

Since Piketty consistently takes the side of bigger government throughout "Cap21," I understand why he prefers tax increases to spending restraint. It is harder, however, to fathom his statement, "if the choice is between a little more inflation and a little more austerity, inflation is no doubt preferable" (page 547). His primary argument is that it is undesirable for the rich to get richer faster than the non-rich, and that government should adopt policies to redistribute more wealth from the rich to the non-rich; yet, as I quoted earlier in this review, Piketty believes that inflation benefits the wealthiest at the expense of the least

---

[45] www.dw.de/eu-governments-cut-deficits-greece-more-than-expected/a-17584652.

wealthy (page 455),[46] so his treatment of inflation is inconsistent, even self-contradictory.

Farther down on page 541 and continuing on the next page, Piketty mentions another potential alternative for reducing government debt—the possibility of privatizing public assets—but he summarily rejects that option due to his unshakable conviction that the government, not private, profit-seeking enterprises, should provide key services such as education and healthcare. Indeed, Piketty himself unwittingly acknowledges that privatization unaccompanied by spending cuts may prove to be insufficient to get the debt problem under control, for, on page 139, he cites what happened in France two decades ago: "the progressive sale of publicly held shares after 1990 brought additional funds into public coffers, although it did not prevent the steady increase in the public debt." In other words, the French government increased spending so rapidly that its budget deficits grew in spite of the additional revenues raised via privatization.

This raises a crucially important problem: If, in fact, Piketty gets his wish, and governments raise taxes in the name of deficit and debt reduction, it will do absolutely nothing to address the persistent budget-busting problem of government spending. Inevitably, sooner or later, government overspending will have to be addressed, but Piketty chooses to ignore this

---

[46] In a confusing, unsupported, unexplained, and seemingly contradictory statement on page 287, Piketty avers that, during wartime at least, "Wages at the bottom of the wage scale ... are somewhat more generously protected from inflation than those at the top."

inescapable reality. In fact, more than merely ignoring the problem of government overspending, he makes a pathetic attempt to win sympathy for governments, writing, "The rich world is rich, but the governments of the rich world are poor" (page 540). Ah yes, Uncle Sam—the impoverished trillionaire, a pitiable pauper. With the ability to spend the incomprehensible sum of nearly $4 trillion per year, surely Piketty can find a more accurate adjective for Uncle Sam than "poor."

There is another particularly glaring omission in "Cap21" in regard to government spending: Piketty doesn't tackle the widespread practice of cronyism. He not only neglects to discuss cronyism, but his blind spot about it renders him oblivious to it. Thus, he writes, "there are two main ways of accumulating wealth: through work or inheritance" (page 379), neglecting to mention a third avenue to riches that many Americans in both the Occupy Wall Street and Tea Party movements find reprehensible—getting rich through government cronyism. Given his concern about the unequal distribution of wealth, it is easy to understand that Piketty would never favor a reduction in government spending that confers benefits on the poor. But why does he maintain a deafening silence about governments giving billions of dollars of handouts to their cronies through corporate welfare, earmarks, etc.? One would assume that he doesn't favor that kind of redistribution, yet he forgoes the opportunity to denounce cronyism and instead elects to skirt the issue entirely.

## 2) The importance of economic growth

A second major blind spot in "Cap21" is the author's failure to offer any detailed suggestions for policies designed to promote economic growth. Piketty acknowledges that slow economic growth is problematical, for he repeatedly laments the consequences of sluggish economic growth: 1) "the return of high capital/income ratios over the past few decades can be explained in large part by the return to a regime of relatively slow growth" (page 25); 2) the growth of large private fortunes in Europe in the early years of the 21st century "is fairly well explained by the lower rate of economic and especially demographic growth in Europe compared with the United States, leading automatically to increased influence of wealth accumulated in the past" (page 154); 3) "in a quasi-stagnant society, wealth accumulated in the past will inevitably acquire disproportionate importance" (page 166).[47] Piketty also perceives that strong economic growth has the opposite effect, the one he desires, commenting, "when growth is high...it is easier for younger generations to accumulate wealth and level the playing field with their elders" (page 400).

Since it is plain that vigorous economic growth is the cure for so much of what Piketty finds undesirable, it is bewildering that he doesn't explore or examine the causes of economic growth. He certainly refers to economic growth frequently, but almost always in the context of quantifying it and reviewing some of growth's ups and downs over the past two centuries. He

---

[47] cf. "Cap21," page 233.

never gets around to explaining how this vitally important phenomenon happens or what policies can be adopted to promote it effectively.

Earlier in this analysis ("Errors of commission" #5), we saw that Piketty has faith in education as the key to long-term economic progress, if not short-term growth. Other than that rather flaccid recommendation, his most detailed pro-growth prescription is this glib, undeveloped, and partially redundant statement near the end of the book: "Growth can of course be encouraged by investing in education, knowledge, and nonpolluting technologies." (page 572)

I already have critiqued his advocacy of education as a key to economic growth, and surely he must be aware of the statistics showing the economically depressive effects of higher-priced, allegedly non-polluting forms of energy. (I say "allegedly" because there really are no non-polluting energy technologies. The manufacturing process for solar panels uses silicon and that for wind-generating turbines uses rare earth metals, while both require massive areas and are devastating to fowl, including some endangered species). The economic mischief of Piketty's preferred energy sources is compounded by the rampant cronyism in those industries, as we have already seen here in the States, with the Obama administration bestowing billions of dollars on green boondoggles[48] that have benefited only political cronies.

---

[48] Mark W. Hendrickson, "Green Fiascoes and Boondoggles," Grove City College, The Center for Vision & Values, November 16, 2011;

3) The role of capital

Piketty actually has another blind spot within his blind spot about growth, and that is the crucial role of capital in economic growth. For a book whose title indicates that the primary subject is capital, Piketty's treatment of capital is strikingly incomplete. He obsesses with measurements about the rate of return to capital and the distribution of capital in different eras and countries, but he never gets around to discussing the economic function of capital nor what factors cause capital to grow.

In fact, Piketty simply takes the growth of capital as a given. He never hints that capital may be increased, decreased, or destroyed, depending on whether it is deployed profitably or unprofitably. Instead, he writes about it using a technique more appropriate to a novelist than an economist—the *deus ex machina*, the unseen supernatural force that somehow mysteriously makes events turn out a certain way. In Piketty's mind, capital is some sort of mysterious, disembodied thing that, thanks to the *deus ex machina* behind the scenes, inexorably grows unless war, taxation, or a deliberate government policy intervenes. Thus: "Very soon, however, [after the end of World War II] capital began to reconstitute itself" (pages 41-2). "Once a fortune is established, the capital grows according to a dynamic of its own, and it can continue to grow at a rapid pace for decades simply because of its size," followed shortly

www.visionandvalues.org/2011/11/green-fiascoes-and-boondoggles/.

by, "Money tends to reproduce itself" (page 440). Also, "the fact remains that beyond a certain threshold, capital tends to reproduce itself and accumulates exponentially" (page 395). Finally, and rather apocalyptically, he avers, "Once constituted, capital reproduces itself faster than output increases. The past devours the future" (page 571).

That last statement is hyperbolic nonsense, mutilating economic reality. Capital doesn't devour the future; it improves and enriches it by multiplying the productivity of labor. If capital were the destructive force that Piketty thinks it is, then wouldn't the last two centuries—the Age of Capitalism—have devastated and impoverished the human race instead of producing unprecedented prosperity of heretofore unimaginable levels of affluence shared by billions of people?

Indeed, Piketty has nothing positive to say about capital. So complete is his blindness to capital's positive contributions to human welfare that when he ventures anywhere near the subject of the functions of capital, he gets it wrong. First, he writes that "speculative bubbles in real estate and stocks have existed as long as capital itself; they are consubstantial with its history" (page 172). Here, Piketty implies that capital causes bubbles. Instead, bubbles (and the eventual bursting of those bubbles) often hurt holders of capital, who are whipsawed by the economic dislocations caused by manipulations of the money supply and interest rates by central banks.[49]

---

[49] Ludwig von Mises, "Human Action (The Scholar's Edition)," Auburn AL: The Ludwig von Mises Institute, 1998, Chapters XVII, XX, and XXXI.

Second, he writes, "Today we know that long-term structural growth is possible only because of productivity growth" (page 228). This is tautological, for improvements in productivity always have driven economic growth. The more wealth an hour of labor produces, the greater, by definition, is the productivity of labor. Productivity gains can come from increased skill and efficiency on the part of the worker, superior management, or additional capital goods made available to the worker.

Historically, additional capital has done the most to boost human productivity: hence, the quantum difference in productivity of a ditch-digger using a shovel and one equipped with a bulldozer.[50] Piketty has it garbled, if not backward, when he asserts, "Only permanent growth of productivity and population can compensate for the permanent addition of new units of capital" (page 228). Improvements in productivity do not happen in spite of additional capital being available, but because of it.

Ultimately, there is a very practical, logical, strategic reason why Piketty gives short shrift to the issue of economic growth. He has painted himself into the proverbial corner by (as explained in "Errors of omission," subsection #1) making government spending cuts off-limits as an option for balancing government budgets.

---

[50] Mises, "The Economic Role of Saving and Capital Goods," The Freeman, August, 1963; www.fee.org/the_freeman/detail/the-economic-role-of-saving-and-capital-goods.

With his brief, perfunctory recommendation for increased government spending on education and nonpolluting technologies, Piketty is paying tepid lip service to the Keynesian doctrine of using government spending to stimulate growth. Prudently, though, he does not venture far out on that thin branch, because the historical evidence is that government stimulus plans fail to restore vigorous economic growth. Huge debt-financed increases in government spending didn't work for Presidents Hoover and Roosevelt in the 1930s[51] nor for Presidents Bush and Obama in the new millennium.

As an erudite scholar, Piketty must be aware that the economic literature documents overwhelmingly that the most effective pro-growth policies are those that shrink governments—preferably by reducing both spending and taxes, but most crucially, by cutting spending.

There are numerous examples[52] from recent years of reductions in government's economic footprint being followed by robust economic growth, and those anecdotal examples are corroborated by comprehensive economic studies by such scholars as economists

---

[51] The term "stimulus" wasn't used in the early 1930s, because the Keynesian Revolution had not yet happened, but clearly Hoover and Roosevelt believed that sluggish private-sector spending must be compensated for by government spending, even if it meant running massive budget deficits.
[52] Mark W. Hendrickson, "Country Economic Policies: What the U.S. Could Learn From Other Countries," Forbes.com, March 12, 2012; www.forbes.com/sites/realspin/2012/03/12/country-economic-policies-what-the-u-s-could-learn-from-other-countries/

Alberto Alesina and Silvia Ardagna,[53] Daniel Oto-Peralías and Diego Romero-Ávila,[54] and Andreas Bergh and Magnus Henrekson[55].

[53] Alberto F. Alesina, Silvia Ardagna, "Large Changes in Fiscal Policiies: Taxes Versus Spending," National Bureau of Economic Research, Paper No. 15438, October 2009; www.nber.org/papers/w15438.

[54] Daniel Oto-Peralías and Diego Romero-Ávila, "Tracing the Link between Government Size and Growth: The Role of Public Sector Quality," International Network for Economic Research, Working Paper 2012.3; www.infer-research.net/upload/WP 2012 3 - Oti-Peralias Romero-Avila.pdf.

[55] Andreas Bergh and Magnus Henrekson, "Government Size and Growth: A Survey and Interpretation of the Evidence," IFN Working Paper No. 858, 2011; www.ifn.se/wfiles/wp/wp858.pdf.

# Part Three:
# The author's biases

Every book reflects its author's beliefs and even his ideology, and "Cap21" is no exception. Here are some of Thomas Piketty's biases:

**Pro-government bias**

1) Double standard regarding competition.

In Piketty's view, private-sector competition is good, but public-sector competition is bad. In making the case for his Number One policy recommendation, a tax on capital, Piketty asserts that such a tax would "promote the general interest over private interests while preserving economic openness and the forces of competition" (page 471). This statement unmistakably shows that he welcomes the disciplining effects of competition on private businesses. He sings a different tune, however, when it comes to competition in the public sector. He writes disapprovingly that "the recent rise of tax competition in the world of free-flowing capital has led many governments to exempt capital income from the progressive income tax"—a competition that he scorns as "an endless race to the bottom" (page 496). He makes the identical characterization of competition between governments that leads to lower corporate taxes (page 562).

Competition works to the benefit of citizens by incentivizing businesses and governments to lower prices. The common problem with government bureaucracies is that they are insulated from competition and consequently operate inefficiently, even wastefully, not as a matter of deliberate choice, but simply in accord with the inherent nature of the bureaucratic model.[56] Piketty, like other statists, consistently prefers key goods and services to be provided by government bureaucracies rather than by private, profit-seeking firms, in spite of the higher costs that bureaucratization imposes on citizens. His opposition to tax competition makes him an advocate for higher taxes; hence, higher costs of living and doing business; hence, lower standards of living.

2) Opposition to privatization.

Similarly, as mentioned above ("Errors of omission, #1) Piketty eschews privatization—the policy of government selling off state-owned enterprises to the private sector—as an option to reduce public debt (page 541). He does so in spite of the fact that Prime Minister Margaret Thatcher's program of privatization[57] succeeded in revitalizing the United Kingdom in the 1980s—a success that was replicated in countries as diverse as Japan, France, India, Australia[58].

---

[56] The theory of bureaucracy is articulated thoroughly and pellucidly in the classic: Ludwig von Mises, "Bureaucracy," 1944; www.mises.org/document/875/Bureaucracy.

[57] Alistair Osborne, "Margaret Thatcher: one policy that led to more than 50 companies being sold or privatized," The Telegraph, April 8, 2013; www.telegraph.co.uk/finance/comment/alistair-osborne/9980292/Margaret-Thatcher-one-policy-that-led-to-more-than-50-companies-being-sold-or-privatised.html.

[58] Madsen Pirie, "Privatization," The Concise Encyclopedia of Economics; www.econlib.org/library/ENc1/Privatization.html.

Piketty assiduously avoids mentioning that the very services he believes must be provided by the public sector—education, health, retirement security, etc. (page 542)—are the very programs that (primarily due to the inherently inefficient nature of bureaucratic management) have caused the current fiscal woes of chronic government deficits and burdensome debt. Indeed, on page 482 Piketty admits, "to be sure, there are objectively growing needs in the educational and health spheres, which may well justify slight tax increases in the future." ("Slight" is a rather disingenuous adjective, given the magnitude of the federal budget deficit here in the States.) The stubborn fact has been that those government-run programs never seem to have enough revenue, yet their advocates keep searching for additional ways to appropriate ever-more wealth from the private sector even as the government's financial condition continues to deteriorate and spiral toward national bankruptcy. It's a shame that Piketty's aversion to the private sector prevents him from recommending a strategy like privatization that eases fiscal pressures by reducing government expenditures while increasing revenues.

3) No government culpability for crisis.

On page 473, Piketty refers to "the structural problems that made the crisis [of 2008-09] possible, including the crying lack of financial transparency and the rise of inequality." As explained above (see Part 2, "Errors of commission"), government's fingerprints were all over the crisis, so for Piketty to cite only nongovernmental causes for the crisis manifests a strong bias.

4) Anti-American bias?

At another point, Piketty takes a passing shot at the U.S., writing that this country "has not always been hailed for international altruism" and "poor countries complain about American stinginess" (page 511). This criticism only appears to be true if one ignores private contributions and defines "altruism" in the artificially narrow sense of "foreign aid dispensed by governments." Although the U.S. leads the world in government-disbursed foreign aid by dollar amount, it is true that in terms of government aid as a percentage of GDP, the U.S. lags well behind other countries. However, in addition to government aid, U.S. citizens, churches, non-profits, foundations, and private businesses annually give massive amounts of aid to foreign recipients—an amount approximately one-and-a-half times as large as Uncle Sam's foreign aid. Private foreign aid from the citizens of other developed countries is minuscule, as a percentage of GDP, by comparison.[59] The bias of counting only government aid as aid unfairly makes the U.S. appear less generous than is actually the case.

5) "Privileges"?

On page 85, Piketty quotes a liberal (in the traditional sense, meaning pro-free market) French economist, Charles Dunoyer, who wrote in 1845, "one consequence of the industrial regime is to destroy artificial inequalities, but this only highlights natural inequalities

[59] "American aid to the developing world"; www.americaintheworld.typepad.com/briefings/2008/08/a merican-aid-to.html.

all the more clearly." Dunoyer opposed government intervention because "superior abilities … are the source of everything that is great and useful … Reduce everything to equality and you will bring everything to a standstill." In rejecting this capitalist ethos, in which market participants prosper in proportion to how much value they provide for their fellow man, Piketty complains, "this argument is often used to justify extreme inequalities and to defend the privileges of the winners."

By "extreme inequalities" he obviously is referring to the large fortunes that accrue to those individuals and enterprises that do the most to satisfy the needs and wants of large numbers of people. Question: Does Piketty want to place an upper limit on how much value people provide to others? Furthermore, his misuse of the word "privileges" shows his pro-government bias. "Privileges" is an apt word to describe the favors (grants, subsidies, etc.) that governments bestow upon cronies and special interest groups—handouts not given to the rest of us.

By contrast, in a free market, nobody "gives" a special favor to a highly successful enterprise. A market-based enterprise is subject to the constant threat of competition from other providers and those enterprises that manage to achieve success in the marketplace earn their fortunes by doing a better job than their competitors of providing value to their customers. Nobody gives them their success; they earn it. Markets don't grant privileges, but governments do. It is an underhanded rhetorical trick to accuse highly profitable entrepreneurs in free markets of having received privileges while ignoring the obvious and glaring injustice of politically connected firms receiving privileges from government.

6) "Favored"?

Similarly, later in "Cap21" Piketty refers to the lower 50 percent of income earners as "the least-favored half of the population" (page 256). This implies, of course, that those in the upper half of income rankings are more favored. But who is doing the favoring? Nobody. Where is the injustice in some people earning more than others? In capitalism, some citizens are naturally more economically productive than others and that is reflected in higher incomes. Again, they didn't receive a favor; their degree of success in providing economic value to others in the competitive marketplace determined their income. Only when government bestows favors on special interests can we rightly speak of some citizens being more-favored. Governments bestow favors; markets do not. Rather, markets unsentimentally and indiscriminately reward those who serve others well and punish those who do not.

7) Who really has "power"?

Piketty worries that those who have more wealth "will have greater power not only over what he or she buys but also over other people: for instance, this person can hire less well-paid individuals to serve his or her needs" (pages 256-7). In the first place, what is wrong with rich people hiring non-rich people to work for them? All jobs, at their root, are work that exists for the purpose of addressing human needs and wants. Would Piketty prefer a person to be unemployed than to work for a rich person?[60] In the second place, Piketty once again uses a term—"power"—that appertains to government, not to private citizens. No private citizen has the power to compel someone to "serve his or her needs." Government, by contrast, routinely compels citizens to surrender a portion of their income so that it can be given to "more-favored" political constituencies who don't provide anything of value (either labor or capital) in exchange for what they receive.[61]

Piketty's paranoia about private power also surfaced in an interview he gave to a New York Times reporter. Then, Piketty expressed his disapproval of tax cuts because they "eventually contribute to rebuild a class of rentiers in the U.S., whereby a small group of wealthy untalented children controls vast segments of the U.S. economy"[62] There are multiple problems with this

---

[60] I think Piketty envisions a nightmare scenario such as existed in the U.S. in the late 1800s when a rich entrepreneur like Andrew Carnegie could find workers to do back-breaking, dangerous work for very low wages. That was possible due to the supply-demand conditions of the era—conditions that, fortunately for workers, have shifted to their benefit. See Mark W. Hendrickson, "In Praise of Capitalist Exploitation," The Center for Vision & Values, March 27, 2009; www.visionandvalues.org/2009/03/in-praise-of-capitalist-exploitation/.

[61] Ostensibly, "unpaid servitude" was outlawed by the Thirteenth Amendment, but obviously the amendment is not strictly enforced.

[57] Piketty interview with Daniel Altman, quoted in Scott Winship, "Whither The Bottom 90 Percent, Thomas Piketty?", Forbes.com April 17, 2014; www.forbes.com/sites/scottwinship/2014/04/17/whither-the-bottom-90-percent-thomas-piketty/.

statement, but I will comment on four: First, the holders of capital in the U.S. today are not "a small group," but number in the millions; second, those who are children in judgment and business sense can lose their capital (yes, some hire expert money managers, but even the most skilled managers are not infallible and sometimes suffer losses); third, the mass of consumers, not the rich minority, determine and control who makes money in a capitalist economy; and fourth, the only "small group of wealthy untalented children [who control] vast segments of the U.S. economy, even though they themselves did little to produce America's vast wealth," is Congress, and Congress, the last time I looked, was a political body, not a free-market, capitalist phenomenon.

8) Who has "rights"?

Piketty's discussion of rights epitomizes his Big Government bias. He writes, "Modern redistribution is built around a logic of rights and a principle of equal access to a certain number of goods deemed to be fundamental" (page 479) and "Modern redistribution…is based on a set of fundamental social rights: to education, health, and retirement" (page 481). In other words, because Piketty embraces the principle that individuals have the right to have certain economic goods, then the state must have the power and access to private wealth necessary for it to provide those goods.

To his credit, he poses the important question, "how far do equal rights extend? … If one includes equal rights to education, health care, and to a pension, as the twentieth-century social state proposed, should one also include rights to culture, housing, and travel?" (page 480) Here Piketty, perhaps unintentionally, exposes the open-endedness, the potential for unlimited expansion, of positive rights—positive rights being a purported right to have something, as opposed to America's traditional negative rights, such as the right not to be killed, not have your property stolen, etc.[63]

Piketty disapproves of "conservative" legal philosophies that recognize individuals as having "fundamental rights with priority over the right of member states to promote the general interests of their people, if need be by levying taxes" (page 567). In this statement, he again uses the word "rights" problematically. He certainly uses it differently than America's founding fathers did. The Ninth and Tenth Amendments to the U.S. Constitution make it plain that the founders understood individual human beings to have certain God-given, inalienable rights; that government is of a different nature, having power, but not rights; that government power is the greatest threat to the rights of people; ergo, government power, and therefore its ability to spend, must be limited—a goal the framers of our constitution sought to attain. Contrariwise, Piketty, consistent with his pro-government bias, exalts government power above individual rights.

[63] Mark W. Hendrickson, "Positive and Negative Government," American Thinker, May 27, 2010; www.americanthinker.com/2010/05/positive_and_negative_governme.html

## Anti-market, anti-capitalism, anti-wealth bias

1) High incomes a no-no

Piketty certainly doesn't disguise his anti-capitalist feelings, charging that incomes above an unspecified point are "excessive" (page 505), "indecent" and "economically useless" (page 473). He sees a silver lining in the two world wars, because they diminished the stock of capital, thereby lessening the degree of inequality in the distribution of wealth. Yet, this so-called improvement, Piketty writes, was, regrettably, temporary, and only "created the illusion that capitalism had been overcome" (page 397).

2) Blaming the free market for government's blunders

Just as Piketty got the history of the Great Depression egregiously wrong by erroneously blaming the free market for the economic discombobulations that government intervention had caused, so he blames the market for government's present-day sins. He writes, "the influence of the state is much greater now than it was then, indeed in many ways greater than it has ever been." And then, in a spectacular non sequitur, he continues, "That is why today's crisis is both an indictment of the markets and a challenge to the role of government" (pages 473-4). He's half right: The crisis (not only the panic of 2008-09, but the subsequent Great Recession and bloated government indebtedness) definitely should cause us to re-examine the role of government. But why should markets be indicted for government's transgressions? Government hasn't given markets a chance to correct the multiple imbalances, malinvestments, and misallocations that have resulted from government having exerted its unprecedented influence to suppress and subvert free markets. It is government intervention (stimulus plans, etc.) that has caused the painful and unnecessary economic stagnation of recent years. It is just as wrong to blame free markets for our current economic woes as it was in the 1930s, because during both periods, government interference with free markets was the true culprit.[64]

3) Using a straw man to disparage free markets

Piketty's anti-market bias is clear in the straw man argument that he sets up when discussing the "right" split between income accruing to capital and to labor. He writes, "Can we be sure that an economy based on the 'free market' and private property always and everywhere leads to an optimal division, as if by magic?" (page 41) Of course not. There is neither utopia nor magic in economics. But Piketty's bias keeps him from questioning whether government overseers and planners know what the "optimal division" between labor and capital is, or whether they have either the wisdom or magical ability to construct an ideal economy.

---

[64] Mark W. Hendrickson, "Blaming the Free Market," and "The Next Great Depression, Updated," The Center for Vision & Values, September 14, 2008 and July 24, 2009, respectively; www.visionandvalues.org/2008/09/blaming-the-free-market/; www.visionandvalues.org/2009/07/the-next-great-depression-updated/.

4) Dismay at the swelling numbers of rich people

Speaking of a widening gap of accumulated wealth between rich and non-rich, the author calls it "even more worrisome than the widening income gap between supermanagers [his term for corporate executives receiving what he considers exorbitant compensation] and others" (page 336). He never identifies or explains what makes this alleged gap "worrisome." Along the same line, Piketty frets that more and more people are receiving inheritances "larger than the least well paid 50 percent of the population earn in a lifetime" (page 420) and calls this "a fairly disturbing form of inequality" (page 421). Most of us, I would think, would prefer there to be a growing number of wealthy individuals. Such a trend represents a democratization of wealth— surely an improvement over the days of a narrow plutocratic elite. But more important is the moral aspect of this situation. Piketty feels that unequal distribution is scandalous, but as long as inherited fortunes were built honestly, what and where is the problem? If a fortune is gained criminally at the expense of the non-rich, that would be a violation of justice and the victims would be entitled to restitution from the rich, but since the large majority of inherited fortunes were gained by delivering value to the non-rich and not by plundering them, there is nothing "worrisome" or morally objectionable about those fortunes.

5) Conflating earned and stolen wealth

Piketty reaches a low point in "Cap21" when he construes a specious equivalence between fortunes gained through theft and those gained honestly in the marketplace. He does this on page 446 where he cites the case of a French court ordering the seizure of part of the fortune of Teodorin Obiang, the son of Equatorial Guinea's dictator, on the grounds that it was booty robbed from the people of his country. After making the sardonic comment that "private property is not quite as sacred as people sometimes think," Piketty proposes a tax on everyone's capital on the utilitarian grounds that a tax would be a more effective way than judicial proceedings to claw back the "ill-gotten gains or unjustified wealth" of thieves.

While it is undeniably true that many crooks evade justice and keep their loot, the imposition of a tax that would cast a wide net and ensnare innocent and guilty individuals indiscriminately is the wrong response. Retrieving the loot of thieves is rightly the job of the courts, not the tax collectors, and for at least two important reasons: 1) a court verdict hits only the perpetrators of crime, and 2) whatever property is recovered through a judicial proceeding is restored to its rightful owners. A general tax on wealth, by contrast, hits a larger number of innocent people than criminals, and the revenue raised by such a tax goes to the government treasury rather than being returned to those from whom it was plundered.

It is "worrisome," to use one of Piketty's own words, that he takes a subtle dig at the Judeo-Christian morality pertaining to private property. Going back in history at least as far as the time of Moses and the children of Israel (to whom the right of private property was, quite literally, sacred), property rights have included the right to restitution—the right of lawful owners to recover property stolen from them. It is disturbing that Piketty proposes a tax that would confer upon government a windfall share of ill-gotten gains while also bypassing the regular legal system that, when successful, delivers restitution and justice to the victims of plunder. For an author who professes a concern for justice to recommend a tax on honest people because it would confiscate a portion of the loot stolen by a much smaller number of people shows a profound disrespect for law-abiding citizens. For him to construe a moral equivalence between wealth earned from voluntary, positive-sum transactions in the marketplace and involuntary, zero-sum, criminal expropriations of property indicates a moral blind spot.

**Collectivist proclivities: vestiges of Marx, centralized control, one-world government**

Thomas Piketty's biases and blind spots are not random nor do they occur in a void; rather, they are determined by his worldview—his ideas, ideologies, and intellectual influences.

1) Vestiges of Marx

Echoes of Marx crop up from time to time in the pages of "Cap21." This is not to say that Thomas Piketty is a dyed-in-the-wool Marxist or a slavish devotee of Marx, for on page 10 of "Cap21," he singles out several errors that Marx had made. On the other hand, though, he embraces at least a partially Marxian framework, for after pointing out a few of Marx's errors, he continues,

"Despite these limitations, Marx's analysis remains relevant in several respects"; "economists today would do well to take inspiration from his example"; and he salutes Marx for "a key insight" (page 10). As we saw earlier (see "Errors of commission," #2) Piketty appears to be under the sway of the labor theory of value—one of the principal pillars of Karl Marx's doctrines. In addition to his affinity for the labor theory, Piketty's worldview resembles Marx's in several noticeable ways.

a) History as quasi-deity

Like Marx, Piketty has a tendency to reify and deify history. Marx firmly believed that "History" is a quasi-deific force that dictates destiny and that History's march in a particular direction is preordained and inexorable. That concept of history leads Piketty to declare that the welfare states built in the 20$^{th}$ century "marked an immense step forward in historical terms" (page 481).

Elsewhere, Piketty's faith in History leads him to make this sweeping unproven pronouncement: "History shows that only countries that are catching up with more advanced economies—such as Europe during the three decades after World War II or China and other emerging countries today—can grow at [a four or five percent rate]" (page 572). There is no *a priori* reason why growth rates can't be higher. Economic modernity is less than three centuries old; it is premature to claim that history or anything else has revealed to us the maximum potential economic growth rate. Today we have access to unprecedented technological marvels, but economic growth has been hobbled by many government obstacles: the liquidation of large amounts of private capital to finance the crony/welfare state via taxation, borrowing, and inflation; the diversion of massive amounts of wealth from the private to the public sector; the crippling of wealth-creating businesses with suffocating regulations.[65] Remove those impediments and with today's technology, and who can say that growth wouldn't take off at unprecedented rates?

b) Grand utopianism

In another chapter, Piketty eerily echoes Marx's utopianism. Marx (with Engels) wrote in "The German Ideology," "In communist society, where nobody has one exclusive sphere of activity but each can become accomplished in any branch he wishes, society regulates the general production and thus makes it possible for me to do one thing today and another tomorrow, to hunt in the morning, fish in the

---

[65] Mark J. Perry, "Federal regulations have lowered real GDP growth by 2 percent per year since 1949 and made America 72 percent poorer," American Enterprise Institute, June 27, 2014; www.aei-ideas.org/2013/06/federal-regulations-have-lowered-gdp-growth-by-2-per-year/ ; cf. www.centerforregulatorysolutions.org/fact-of-the-day-january-24-2014/.

afternoon, rear cattle in the evening or criticize after dinner, just as I desire." This is Piketty's version: "We are free to imagine an ideal society in which all other tasks are almost totally automated and each individual has as much freedom as possible to pursue the goods of education, culture, and health for the benefit of herself and others. Everyone would be by turns teacher or student, writer or reader, actor or spectator, doctor or patient" (page 308). For supposedly writing "scientific" texts, both authors share a weakness for grandiose utopian visions.

Piketty's idealism occasionally leads him to indulge utopian fantasy, most noticeably when he writes, "In theory, of course, there is no reason why a country cannot decide to devote two-thirds or three-quarters of its national income to taxes, assuming that taxes are collected in a transparent and efficient manner and used for purposes that everyone agrees are of high priority" (page 481). "Everyone agrees?" In our world populated by willful human beings? In our democracies filled with special interest groups, each tugging in its own direction? Sorry, but no society will ever come close to having everyone agree on what government's priorities should be.

c) Illiberal democracy

Piketty shares the Marxian sense of democracy—the simple majoritarianism whereby when two foxes and one chicken vote on what to have for lunch, the outcome is predetermined. Seen in that light, we can see why Marx enthusiastically embraced democracy. He believed that a democratic majority would succeed in appropriating the property of the rich, thereby ushering in socialism.[66] Similarly, Lenin wrote approvingly, "A democracy is a state which recognizes the subjection of the minority to the majority."[67] America's founding fathers, most famously, John Adams and James Madison,[68] abhorred the illiberal tendencies of democracy quite vigorously. That is why no form of the word "democracy" appears in our founding documents (i.e., Declaration of Independence, Constitution, Bill of Rights). The American system of government was designed to insulate us from the predations of democracy.

Piketty clearly comes down on the Marxian side of the democratic divide. He writes, "One of the most important issues in coming years will be the development of new forms of property and

---

[66] See "The Communist Manifesto," Chapter 2; https://www.marxists.org/archive/marx/works/1848/communist-manifesto/cho2.htm.

[67] Nikolai Lenin, "The State and Revolution," included in "A New Dictionary of Quotations on Historical Principles from Ancient and Modern Sources" sel. and ed. by H.L. Mencken, New York: Alfred A. Knopf, 1942, p. 277.

[68] Adams: "Democracy never lasts long. It soon wastes, exhausts and murders itself" (in a letter to John Taylor, 1814); Madison: "Democracy is the most vile form of government" (Federalist Paper #10).

democratic control of capital" (page 569); "If we are to regain control of capitalism, we must bet everything on democracy" (page 573); and "If necessary, the tax can be quite steeply progressive on very large fortunes, but this is a matter for democratic debate under a government of laws" (page 532). The stipulated condition of "democratic debate" may sound perfectly reasonable, but Piketty is counting on there being more non-rich, anti-rich votes than pro-rich. To give him the benefit of the doubt, his idealism prevents him from seeing that a government powerful enough to redistribute wealth for social welfare purposes is also strong enough to—and in practice virtually always will—channel wealth to well-heeled cronies, too.

2) Collectivist central planning

"Cap21" is sprinkled with holistic terms that betray a collectivistic mindset—e.g., "Europe might find" (page 546); "Europe created" (pages 556-7); "no reason why a country can't decide" (page 481); "countries willing to accept such a tax" (page 471); "a more just and rational social order based on common utility" (page 234); "the material conditions that different countries decide to provide" (page 80).

Holistic language goes hand-in-hand with collectivistic policy preferences, such as, "it is vital to make sure that social inequalities derive from rational and universal principles rather than arbitrary contingencies.

**86**

Inequalities must therefore be just and useful to all" (page 422).

Piketty uses the term "general interest" as a synonym for the "collective interest" to which the welfare and rights of individual citizens should be sacrificed for the greater good. Thus, he advocates "a tax on capital [because it] would promote the general interest over private interests" (page 471). As mentioned above (see "A pro-government bias"), Piketty objects to a conservative interpretation of individual rights when those rights interfere with the ability "of member states to promote the general interest of their people" (page 567).

In regard to central bank intervention to bail out a stressed corporation or financial institution, Piketty writes, "If the loan initiated by the central bank enables the recipient to escape from a bad pass and avoid a final collapse (which might decrease the national wealth), then, when the situation has been stabilized and the loan repaid, it makes sense to think that the loan from the Fed increased the national wealth (or at any rate prevented national wealth from decreasing)" (page 550). Similarly, "If private investors are unwilling to spend and invest, why shouldn't governments invest?" (page 568)

Apart from the fact that government officials and central bankers lack the specific knowledge to pinch-hit successfully for private citizens who do have that knowledge, public officials tend not to invest public monies (a/k/a others people's money) as carefully as individuals invest their own. Piketty's statements imply that public-sector "experts" have the wisdom to see which companies should be propped up and which should be allowed to fail. This is the essence of the central economic planning that failed so abysmally in the old Soviet Union. Central planners are poor substitutes for free markets, as Piketty himself acknowledges in his statement that central bankers "can also be very wrong in their choice of targets" (page 552). This is one of several occasions in "Cap21," in which Piketty employs the slick politician's tactic of speaking out of both sides of his mouth at different places, using ambivalence to create the impression that he is a moderate who agrees at least in part with everyone. On the issue of economic planning by the powers that be, the preponderance of evidence places him unmistakably on the side of statist intervention and elitist control.

3) Visions of one-world governance

Although he never explicitly announces it, it seems that Piketty eventually would like to see a global government. Until then, though, the "ideal policy for avoiding an endless inegalitarian spiral and regaining control over the dynamics of accumulation would be a progressive global tax on capital." He does concede, however, that, at this point in time, "a truly global tax on capital is no doubt a utopian ideal" (page 471).

A few pages later, he provides a more explicit glimpse of his desire for a worldwide government: "it will be impossible to convince a majority of citizens that our governing institutions (especially at the supranational level) need new tools unless the instruments already in place can be shown to be working properly" (page 474). "Admittedly, a global tax on capital would require a very high and no doubt unrealistic level of international cooperation. But countries wishing to move in this direction could very well do so incrementally" (page 515). The collectivistic central planner in him re-emerges when he writes, "a global tax on capital … has the merit of preserving economic openness while effectively regulating the global economy and justly distributing the benefits among and within nations" (page 516). He never ventures to tell us exactly who would actually determine what a supposedly "just" distribution of wealth would be.

There are practical economic problems associated with a global wealth tax beyond the formidable political challenge of getting all the governments of the world to cooperate on its implementation and enforcement. The major difficulty is the same one that arises when inheritance taxes are levied: Not all wealth sits in liquid forms; consequently, the tax-enforced need to raise cash can be very disruptive, sometimes making it necessary for businesses and enterprises to dismember themselves or even liquidate.

The reader should find Piketty's proposal to tax accumulated wealth at very small percentages less than reassuring. He writes innocuously, "One might imagine a rate of 0 percent for net assets below 1 million euros, 1 percent between 1 and 5 million, and two percent above 5 million" with maybe "0.1 percent below 200,000 euros" (page 517). The stipulation of "net assets" is problematical. If he is proposing here to give a tax break to those who are heavily in debt, then the debt problem surely would worsen because granting tax exemptions for debts creates an incentive to incur debt.

Before one is tempted to jump on the wealth tax bandwagon because Piketty is talking about a top rate of only two percent, consider the history of the American graduated income tax. One of the selling points for the adoption of the 16th Amendment to the Constitution was the promise that it would have a top rate of only 7 percent, and only on very high incomes. Within a mere five years, though, Congress raised the top rate from 7 percent to 77 percent and also increased rates on more modest incomes.

It is not hard to imagine a similar dynamic if a progressive tax on wealth (either national or global) were adopted. In fact, Piketty himself reveals that he has higher rates in mind, for he writes, "To obtain one-time receipts of 20 percent of GDP, it would therefore suffice to apply a special levy …10 percent between 1 and 5 million and 20 percent above 5 million" (page 544). Given government debts in the vicinity of 100 percent of GDP and the inability of democratic governments to control spending, to consider Piketty's "special levy" a one-off event might be a matter of self-delusion or wishful thinking. Considering that he also believes that "the optimal [income] tax rate in the developed countries is probably above 80 percent" (page 512) starting on incomes as low as $500,000 per year (page 513), it's hard to imagine that he wouldn't start calling for higher tax rates on accumulated wealth once such a tax is in place.

Readers in the Middle East might be particularly interested in these ideas in "Cap21": "When it comes to regulating global capitalism and the inequalities it generates, the geographic distribution of natural resources and especially of 'petroleum rents' constitutes a special problem…If the world were a single global democratic community, an ideal capital tax would redistribute petroleum rents in an equitable manner." There's the central planner surfacing again, but the author hastens to allay any concerns by reassuring us with the modest disclaimer, "It is not up to me to calculate the optimal schedule for the tax on petroleum capital that would ideally exist in a global political community based on social justice and utility" (page 537). But apparently Piketty believes that whoever oversees the redistribution of wealth globally would "achieve a more just distribution of petroleum rents, be it by way of sanctions, taxes, or foreign aid in order to give countries without oil the opportunity to develop" (page 538).

Another aspect of the collectivist framework and utopian notion of worldwide unity (both political and intellectual) that infuses "Cap21" surfaces when the author writes, "One might hope, moreover, that immigration will be more readily accepted by the less advantaged members of the wealthier societies if such institutions are in place to ensure that the economic benefits of globalization are shared by everyone" (page 539). It is amazing how in one breezy sentence, Piketty makes it sound like certain unnamed planners will be able to create institutions that would be able to guarantee a political system that would be able to redistribute global wealth to the satisfaction of everyone.

Another example of Piketty's supra-sovereign (some would say, "anti-sovereign") one-world idealism is the following plan he proposes: "Monetary union is supposed to lead naturally to political, fiscal, and budgetary union, to ever closer cooperation among the member states" (page 556). To achieve greater political integration of European countries, he recommends that the euro zone governments "pool their public debts" (page 558). Then, "to decide how quickly to pay down the pooled debt, or, in other words, to decide how much public debt the Eurozone should carry, one would need to empower a European 'budgetary parliament' to decide on a European budget. The best way to do this would be to draw the members of this parliament from the ranks of the national parliaments, so that European parliamentary sovereignty would rest on the legitimacy of democratically elected national assemblies. Like any other parliament, this body would decide issues by majority vote after open public debate" (page 559).

Realistically, though, how democratic—in the sense of representing the desires of the voters—would a parliament be if its members were to be elected by members of national parliaments? From everything I've read and heard, Europeans already feel that those who sit on the European Council, the European Commission, and the Council of the European Union are remote and unaccountable to them. In practice, governing bodies consisting of politicians selected by politicians are elitist in nature, though masquerading as democratic.

Piketty outlines a scenario in which Europe would operate "with a budget deficit limited to 1 percent of GDP" (page 545). Besides reeking of top-down planning, this scenario completely discounts the practical difficulties of maintaining budget discipline in a welfare state in which massive amounts of wealth are up for grabs in the democratic process. It ignores the inconvenient fact that numerous European governments already have broken their solemn promises to keep their budget deficits within specified limits as a condition of their membership in the EU.

Piketty writes, "In an ideal society, what level of public debt is desirable? Let me say at once that there is no certainty about the answer [nice of him to admit this], and only democratic deliberation [foxes and chickens again] can decide, in keeping with the goals each society [holistic terminology again] sets for itself" (page 562). His idealistic and collectivistic worldview is unmistakable. Other collectivists will embrace him; those who believe in individual rights and liberty see a dangerous threat.

# Part Four: Closing thoughts

## A few words about the quality of writing

Since this is a book review, let me offer some insights into how well written the book is. Let's start with a compliment: Overall, the prose in "Cap21" is quite readable. Other than a relatively few paragraphs that may prove challenging for readers not accustomed to dealing with symbols (simple equations consisting of primarily Latin letters, with a couple of Greek letters thrown in for fun), Piketty's prose is fluent and generally clear.

This is not to say that the writing is without flaws. The biggest problem is that "Cap21," a long book by necessity due to all the historical discussions and data included, is, regrettably, longer than it needs to be. There is too much nonessential verbal padding. In places, the exposition is bloated, pedantic, and meandering. This subtracts from optimal reader-friendliness. Here I am inclined to blame Piketty's editor(s) more than the author himself. The flaws fall into five categories:

1) The cross-referencing within the book is frustrating. Numerous times Piketty writes that he will elaborate on a point later, or he refers to passages that occurred earlier in the book, without specifying the pages. Consequently, the reader has to take time to hunt them down. For example, on page 431 he writes, "In view of the law of compound interest discussed in Chapter 1…" Alas, the book's index omits "compound interest," and I failed to locate the passage with a cursory flip through the pages of Chapter 1. It would have been very helpful if the editor had inserted the pertinent page numbers

after each cross-reference—e.g., (pages 1-5) or (see page 400).

2) The text is littered with too many banal and trite truisms that should have been omitted edited out of the text. For example, on page 553 we read, "when significant shares of national wealth are shifted about, it is best not to make mistakes." Gee, do you think so? (Pardon the sarcasm, but I just couldn't resist.) Another example: "In practice, financial institutions and stock markets are generally a long way from achieving this ideal of perfection" (page 214). And then there is this gem: "United Nations forecasts are not certainties" (page 81).[69]

3) For a work trumpeted as a paragon of thorough scholarship and research, "Cap21" contains a surprising number of unfounded assertions and arbitrary opinions. Perhaps not surprisingly, the exaggerated and/or dubious statements are concentrated in the latter portions of the book, where Piketty argues for particular policies. Here are just a few examples: "In the long run, unequal wealth within nations is surely more worrisome than unequal wealth between nations" (page 432); "past a certain threshold, all large fortunes, whether inherited or entrepreneurial in origin, grow at extremely high rates" (page 439); "every fortune is partially justified

---

[69] There are also a couple of sentences that make no sense at all. I wonder if they are rare mistakes in what appears to be an excellent English translation by Arthur Goldhammer: "a country in which people die older is very different from a society in which they don't die at all" (page 390) and ""the dead have always been (on average) wealthier than the living in France." (page 391)

yet potentially excessive" (page 444); "the unlimited growth of global inequality of wealth…is currently increasing at a rate that cannot be sustained in the long run" (page 572). Other examples of Piketty's unfounded sweeping assertions are scattered throughout this review.

4) The repeated disclaimers and qualifications about his data being admittedly incomplete or his classifications or designations being arbitrary are tiresome. On the one hand, I appreciate his honesty, but I think his statement on page 571 is sufficient: "The sources on which this book draws are more extensive than any previous author has assembled, but they remain imperfect and incomplete. All of my conclusions are by nature tenuous and deserve to be questioned and debated." As discussed in Part One above, "Piketty's magic trick," his faulty data succeeded in luring others into a diversionary debate about measurements of inequality.

5) "Cap21" goes to the proverbial well too often in making allusions to various novels and TV shows. In particular, he repeatedly uses the novels of Jane Austen and Honoré de Balzac to illustrate the rigid economic realities that prevailed in France and England at the dawn of the 19th century. The first time or two that Piketty takes us on this literary journey are enjoyable. By the fourth or fifth time, though, they become tiresome and bog down the narration.

**The reader's verdict**:

Does "Cap21" deserve the acclaim it has received? The answer to that question, I suspect, depends on whether one shares Piketty's biases, adheres to his egalitarian philosophy, and is willing to overlook the not-insignificant number of economic fallacies the author uses to buttress his thesis. Those who share the author's belief that governments should do even more to redistribute wealth are likely to praise the book, while those who are not so inclined will find little to like about it. With dubious and discredited data along with meandering organization and other flaws cited in the previous section, even the book's fans would be hard-pressed to call it a masterpiece. Its timing is opportune, even fortuitous, for certain political and ideological partisans.

"Cap21"'s argument for an egalitarian redistribution of wealth places it at political stage center here in the States. Indeed, the stakes in this debate are immense. Thomas Piketty has made his case for a greater degree of egalitarian redistribution. I have tried to expose some of the flaws in his argument, and to encourage us not to sacrifice liberty and prosperity to the ideology of egalitarianism. And now, dear reader, it is up to you to choose where you stand on this defining political issue.

# About the Author

Dr. Mark Hendrickson is an adjunct professor of economics at Grove City College, where he has taught since 2004. He is also a Fellow for Economic and Social Policy with The Center for Vision & Values, for which he writes regular commentaries. He is a contributing editor of The St. Croix Review and TheMoralLiberal.com, sits on the Council of Scholars of the Commonwealth Foundation, and writes the "No Panaceas" column in the Op/Ed section of Forbes.com.

After completing his B.A. in Spanish from Albion College, he at various times studied at the University of Michigan School of Law, Oxford University (Shakespeare and world literature), and Harvard (moral education) before earning his masters and doctorate degrees under the tutelage of the late economist and Grove City College icon, Dr. Hans F. Sennholz.

His published books include: "America's March Toward Communism" (1987)—a study of the extent to which Karl Marx' ten point-platform for socializing an economy has been implemented in the United States; "The Morality of Capitalism" (editor, 1992); "Famous But Nameless: Inspiration and Lessons from the Bible's Anonymous Characters" (2011); and "God and Man on Wall Street: The Conscience of Capitalism" (with Craig Columbus, 2012). His commentaries have been published in The Freeman, Reason, New Guard, Human Events, The Washington Times, The Washington Examiner, The Christian Science Monitor,

AmericanThinker.com, and USAToday.com, among others.

Hendrickson lives with his wife Eileen in Amish country near Grove City.